Forgiving Kevin

*A Son's Addiction Becomes a
Father's Greatest Teacher*

Larry Glenz

BALBOA.
PRESS

A DIVISION OF HAY HOUSE

ISBN: 978-1-4525-3810-5 (sc)
ISBN: 978-1-4525-3809-9 (e)
ISBN: 978-1-4525-3811-2 (hc)
Library of Congress Control Number: 2011917246

Balboa Press books may be ordered through booksellers or by contacting:

Balboa Press
A Division of Hay House
1663 Liberty Drive
Bloomington, IN 47403
www.balboapress.com
1-(877) 407-4847

Printed in the United States of America
Balboa Press rev. date: 9/28/2012

Preface

In this world, bad things happen to good people. It takes right-minded perception to be able to handle life's most difficult challenges. Turning to one's Higher Power, Holy Spirit, Divine Guidance, or any other term that is comfortable, is the path that gives the strength needed.

The story of Kevin's addiction to drugs and the consequences that accompany it, unfortunately, is not uncommon. Trusting God or Spirit to give strength during the difficult times is not easy. Our fears often get the better of us and we react in an unloving way. This exacerbates the problem, making the addict and those who love him miserable.

Not everyone in the field of drug rehabilitation agrees on how the loved ones of an addict should behave. One theory is that the parents must use all the "leverage" they have to force the addict into recovery. Since addiction to these powerful drugs always progresses, it is deemed necessary to use any method at one's disposal to get the addict into treatment. It is a dangerous game the addict plays and those who love him are responsible to do all in their power to save his life.

Another theory says that we are powerless over another's addiction. We can offer help but forcing the addict into treatment against his will is unproductive. No rehab can help an addict if he is not ready to accept treatment. The loved ones, however, can learn that they can experience serenity and even happiness whether the addict is active or not. Turning to one's Higher Power during these tough times will never guarantee the outcome of sobriety but it does provide the strength to handle whatever comes.

My story as Kevin's father provides a memoir of my struggle to stay with the advice of Spirit during his seven-year ordeal of opiate addiction. My contemplations with Holy Spirit are documented from my personal journals and are presented exactly as I received the advice from my Higher Power. But often my fears led me away from the advice of Spirit and I used guilt and shame to try and get my son to stop. Although Spirit's advice was consistent, my actions were not.

This account of Kevin and me is true with name changes for all those except the people within the circle of our family. I am not certain exactly what it teaches—but I'm hoping the message that comes from this book is that only the love matters in any situation.

Kevin and I talked often of what a help he could be to other addicts as a sponsor or even as an addiction counselor. My hope now is that our story can inspire others to turn to the true Source of strength and wisdom while confronting life's most difficult challenges.

I see the story of Kevin and me as a love story. When **not** seen through the prism of metaphysical truths, it is a sad and frightening story. However, all love is eternal and I carry this love with me wherever I go and to whomever I meet. **And love is all that matters.**

Chapter 1 –
Can You Get Us Through This One?

⟞⟐⟞⟐⟞⟐⟝

I was sitting in the doctor's office with my mom when the first call came. My mom had recently been diagnosed with cancer and my brother Mike and I were there for support. I didn't recognize the number so I took my time before I stepped outside to hear the message of the caller. It was strange. I heard a lot of shouts and noises that I couldn't understand but I also heard the caller say in an unsettled voice, "Mr. Glenz?" The phone message cut out abruptly and I was left to wonder what that was all about. I decided to let that go for the time being.

Ten minutes later, I felt the vibration of the cell phone in my pocket. This time it was Joe Renken, the Assistant Principal of Sherwood HS where I worked as a long tenured teacher and coach. Joe was a great friend, my former assistant lacrosse coach and a special colleague of mine. But I felt this was serious business with the doctor and my mom so I did not pick up the call. When I finally stepped outside to hear the voice message, Joe had said it was urgent that I get back to him. I called back immediately.

In a calm voice Joe said he received a call from Tim Curcio, a NYC cop and former lacrosse player of mine and Joe's on the first of our two NY State Championship teams in 1999. Tim had called the high school looking for me but asked for Coach Renken when told I was out of the school. Joe said there was no reason to panic but my son, Kevin, was found passed out on the pavement of a gas station somewhere in Brooklyn. He was now in Wycoff Hospital on the Brooklyn—Queens border and it looked like he was going to be okay. "What happened?" I asked. "Was he hit by a car?" Joe paused before he said softly, "Tim's pretty sure it was a drug overdose. He got him to the hospital quickly and will be there if you go now."

I asked my brother to take our mom back to her home at the Atlantic Assisted Living Facility without explaining anything to them. I got Tim's number and called him on the way to the city. After reassuring me that Kevin would be okay, he explained that he responded to a call from a gas station owner that complained of a wild man in convulsions on his property. When Officer Curcio and his partner arrived they found the body faced down, out cold and his face was blue. He checked the vital signs and he was breathing with a pulse but he looked ghastly and was unconscious. When checking the victim's identification, Tim was chilled to the bone when he realized that this was actually his former teammate from high school—his coach's son—and sort of a friend.

Tim had found other junkies in similar condition in this area of Brooklyn but he later confided, "It shakes you up to find out it is one of your own." After he called for an ambulance, he called Sherwood HS. When he got my cell number and called, he might have thought it was better to not leave a message until he knew if Kevin would make it out of the coma. The ambulance had just arrived so he called Sherwood HS again and asked Mr. Renken to get in touch with me and gave his cell number.

What were the chances that of the tens of thousands of New York City policemen, the one who would find Kevin would be perhaps the only one of the entire NYPD who knew him? What was he doing in Brooklyn anyway? Kevin lived in Merrick on Long Island with his mother. I had actually talked to Kevin an hour earlier when I went to pick up his grandmother for the doctor's appointment and he seemed fine. He said something about being on a new job. Tim said he was wearing a Verizon nametag on his shirt when he found him. Apparently, Kevin had just started a new job with the phone company.

As it turns out, Kevin had just shot up a large quantity of heroin in a car while parked in the gas station. He was with another guy on the job. When Kevin overdosed, the kid panicked and fled in the car leaving him on the ground in convulsions. Officer Tim Curcio rode in the ambulance and was with him when I called and said Kevin appeared stable. I told him I'd be there as fast as I could. The ride to Brooklyn was thick with traffic and my mind turned to the Holy Spirit with prayer. "Can you get us through this one?" I asked.

****

The emergency room of Wycoff hospital was totally chaotic—overcrowded, crazy, loud, and full of every ethnic face and costume imaginable. I was allowed in to see Kevin but had trouble finding him. The staff looked as frazzled as the patients and families of these ill and injured people; yet I will always be eternally grateful to the doctors and nurses who took care of Kevin that day.

I found Kevin on a cot behind a blue curtain with an IV in his arm, eyes closed and his mouth wide open. I stood there looking at him for a long while, wondering how things ever got this far. He awoke slightly when the doctor was tending to him. His eyes caught mine; then he vomited violently into a plastic container next to the cot. The doctor asked him how many bags he had done. Kevin looked totally incoherent but somehow managed to answer, "One." Drug addicts always lie instinctively, even when wiped out and it's to no advantage. Drugs and lies always coincide.

Officer Curcio showed up again in his uniform at the end of his shift. He seemed pretty uncomfortable seeing me in this situation. We had all shared some of the most glorious of times together in our roles as coach and player a few years back. And this was the lowest point we had experienced together for sure. I got a chance to hug and thank him personally. When Tim said goodbye to Kevin, he threw up again. In fact, he continued puking all the way home in my car. I took him straight to his mother's house and he went right to bed. My ex-wife, CB, was upset at me for not keeping her better informed about his condition over the six hours since I called her to tell her Kevin had OD'ed. I could have and should have been more compassionate towards her. This was tough on all of us. But this wasn't the beginning and it wouldn't be the end of this drug horror—not by a long shot.

****

Chapter 2 –
A New Arrangement

H ow does an All-American boy like Kevin become a heroin addict? Kevin was the kind of kid you dream about—good looking, athletic, high achiever in school, lots of friends, big personality. Although he was labeled in 1st grade as "Learning Disabled," his strong work ethic allowed him to receive outstanding grades. He never missed a day of school or even a homework assignment. The "LD" label gave him many benefits toward achieving high grades. He received lots of help from Special Education teachers with reading labs, extra time on tests, and preferred schedules. From the earliest time, Kevin was totally determined to be an outstanding student athlete. Both his father and mother were teachers and coaches and the top high school student athletes became his real life heroes.

Although he was somewhat small throughout his school age years, he was fast, strong, tough, agile, and well coordinated. But most of all, he was determined to succeed. Actually, he was too determined. Anytime he was unsuccessful in any endeavor, he either flew into a rage or cried uncontrollably. His competitive instincts were over the top. He challenged his brother, Matt, in everything, even though Matt was 5 years older. Kevin was lucky that Matt was an easy going kid because many older brothers would have given him a beating. Matt rarely did, although in most cases it would have been well deserved.

Like his classmates, Kevin played many sports in grade school. Like most dads, I either coached or attended his events unless I was coaching my own school team at the same time. Getting to see my older son, Matt, play in junior high and high school was tough because it conflicted with my coaching schedule. The youth leagues, however, usually played after 6PM so it was easier to get there because my practice or game was over.

But by the time he entered middle school, Kevin was focused on football, wrestling, and lacrosse—the 3 sports his dad coached and his older brother played. He had attended so many of my games as a young child that he fell in love with the sports, the school, and the players over the years. His brother, Matt, played for Webster HS in the town of Merrick where we lived. But the blue and gray of Webster HS had less of the success than the green and gold clad Sherwood teams in football and lacrosse during Kevin's formative years in the 80's and early 90's.

When CB and I split up in 1994, my mom and I made a decision to buy a house in Sherwood. Matt and Kevin had a choice of which school they would want to attend. Matt was 17 and had established roots at Webster. He also had little desire to be the coach's son with all the added pressure that would entail. Kevin, on the other hand, was 12 and associated Sherwood with winning and had dreamed of wearing green and gold as his high school heroes had through the years. Sherwood and Merrick were less than a 20 minute drive from each other, so despite their parents' separation, the boys would get to easily see each other on a regular basis. Both parents and both kids were happy with this arrangement.

And so was Kevin's grandmother, Nanny, as she was called by her grandkids. My mom was ecstatic at the thought of living with her son and grandson. Kevin could barely control his joy. He was going to go to Sherwood, play for Sherwood, play for his dad, and be spoiled rotten by Nanny. He'd see his mom often and talk to her every day. "What could be better?" he thought.

****

Chapter 3 –
Loving Sherwood

A legal separation between a husband and wife of 19 years is never easy but CB and I wanted to make it as seamless as possible for the kids. We told them about the possibility of moving back together in one of the houses in the future. We even talked to our close friends about this as if something other than the troubles with our marriage was the motivating force behind the move. We stressed how good it would be for my mom, Phyllie, who had lived alone since my father's death three years earlier. Kevin had always wanted to attend Sherwood HS so we presented our separation to others as positive opportunities for everyone. Our marriage had gone bad but CB and I were dressing it up nicely for the kids' sake.

I found a great house located just a stone's throw from the football and lacrosse fields. My mom would take the master bedroom and Kevin and I both had our own rooms on the same floor. There was an apartment downstairs that I could rent or eventually take over for myself. While the idea of living with my mom again at age 44 was unsettling, I never could have pulled off this arrangement of two houses without her. I had used some of her money from the family house we sold after my dad died as a down payment, and I took care of all the bills once we moved in. Phyllie was thrilled to have her old function as master homemaker returned to her. She still missed my dad, but this was a role she loved and lost when he died. She cooked, cleaned, shopped, washed clothes, and scheduled our days with the effectiveness of a corporate secretary.

Kevin, at age 12, started 7th grade at Sherwood Middle School, located less than 100 yards from our front door. The high school where I taught history was a mile up the road so my commute to work was now one or two minutes depending on whether or not I caught the stop light. I was the head coach of the middle school football and the varsity lacrosse teams—both of which played on the fields of Sherwood Middle School. Although I was more shaken by the split with my wife than I let on, it seemed that I had certainly made the best of a bad situation. CB and I had free range to visit each other's houses and the kids seemed not to be badly affected. In fact, it might have been better for there was none of the verbal violence that they experienced with their mom and dad at each other's throats on a daily basis.

Nanny took care of Kevin's every need and this certainly lightened the load of parenting for me. He was punctual and completely prepared for every class, athletic practice, game, or any other commitment. She prepared all his meals to his specific liking whenever he wanted. His clothes were laid out for him every day. Nanny drove him in her car wherever and whenever he wanted or needed to go. Without exception, Kevin was the first thing she thought about when she awoke and the last thing before she fell asleep. And she was thrilled with the situation. "A new lease on life", she called it.

****

Kevin thrived from the outset. He knew some kids already from coming to so many games and had participated occasionally in some of the youth programs in wrestling and lacrosse starting at about 6 years old. He loved going to Sherwood Middle School and playing middle school football for Sherwood. I was the head coach with my long time assistant, Tom Storm, and my partner in both football and lacrosse, Bill Greeley. We had a very good team. In fact, in the two years that Kevin played middle school football we never lost a game. Kevin was a fine tail back and was our most effective ball carrier. He was small but fast, tough and always ran to daylight. He never got hurt or had to come off the field. He was totally dedicated and excited to be in this situation—winning every game, scoring touchdowns, gaining big chunks of yardage, making tackles on defense, and having the time of his life. We'd walk home to a dinner that Phyllie had prepared for us. My assistant coach, Bill Greeley, was a young bachelor and Phyllie loved to have him come for dinner. Phyllie or I would help Kevin with his homework and, with the help of his Special Education teachers, he was on the honor roll for every report card.

Still, there was something unusual or unnatural about the anxiety Kevin felt about succeeding. If he had trouble with a test, he would be a wreck all night over it. If he fumbled a football or if someone else starred in a game instead of him, he'd brood about it for long periods of time. He couldn't sleep alone without being scared and would run into Nanny's room in the middle of the night to go to sleep on the floor of her bedroom almost every night. He worried about everything in what appeared to be an unhealthy way. His temper toward Nanny or me was often uncontrollable and he would be disrespectful to both of us when everything wasn't going exactly as he wished.

The teachers at school and the parents of his friends all raved about how wonderful, polite, and engaging he was, so his behavior and attitude in the house was all the more confusing. Nanny wasn't used to being treated with the disrespect that Kevin would lash out at her with. Neither my brother Mike nor I would have ever dared to talk to her like that when we were his age. She called him "street angel / house devil." But he only seemed to get worse if he was punished for his bad behavior. Both Phyllie and I were frustrated but this wasn't really anything that was new to me. His mom always had trouble controlling him or disciplining his temper. CB might have even been secretly pleased that Nanny could do no better. Kevin was tough to handle among the family whether he was treated gently or roughly.

He never seemed to show this side to others, however. I took him to a child psychologist to see if there was some answer to this anxiety, frustration, and anger that he would unleash on us. But like others on the outside, the psychologist also found him charming and delightful. In fact, when Kevin told the psychologist that I had hit him for being disrespectful, the doctor threatened to report me to the authorities for child abuse. Hitting him or taking privileges away from him rarely worked anyway. He admitted he would purposely provoke me to hit him by saying the most disrespectful comments he could think of so that I would be in the wrong more than him. His Nanny was frustrated but also quick to forgive. Nothing seemed to work as far as getting respectful behavior when he was in one of his moods.

So the appearance to the Sherwood community was that Kevin was a happy, polite, friendly, high achieving "wonder boy". Since lots of parents and teachers complained about the disrespect of teenagers, I didn't want to make too big a deal out of this. After all, considering the family had been broken in half by the separation of his parents, most things were going quite well. Like his brother Matt said, "Kevin has always been crazy. Nanny never knew because she never lived with him." There seemed to be a lot of truth in that.

****

Chapter 4 –
Early Sherwood Years

For the first four years that Kevin lived and went to school in Sherwood, he was an unqualified success academically. Because of his status as Learning Disabled (LD), he received special attention with his scheduling. He was exempt from taking a foreign language, his teachers were carefully selected, and the Special Education teachers saw him daily in the reading lab to monitor his progress. His grandmother was on top of every assignment that was due and was attuned to any concern or difficulty the boy might have in his studies. If Phyllie didn't think she was able to be of necessary help, she would bring it to my attention. If I couldn't help, I would find the right faculty member to direct me to the best way for him to succeed. Kevin's desire to be an impressive student athlete was consistent. His attendance and his record of completing his homework assignments were near perfect. His grade point average was above 90 and he was always on the honor roll.

In athletics, he was even more impressive. He played three sports: football, wrestling, and lacrosse. Football became a challenge once he hit the junior varsity, however, because he was considerably smaller than most of the players. At less than 110 lbs. he was no longer one of the team's top players, but he did see playing time and contributed to the team's success. He remained quick, tough, and talented. Once he grew, it was reasonably expected that he would be an important asset to the program on varsity. As it turned out, he was.

As a freshman and sophomore, Kevin was already a varsity wrestler and lacrosse player. He seemed to have natural qualities as a wrestler. He could physically overpower the kids in his weight class of 105 lbs. and he had excellent balance and agility. His learning disability seemed to affect him in this sport, however. Kevin never really learned the intricacies of wrestling, despite the fact that he started wrestling at the earliest age. Although we had wrestling mats in our basement and rolled around wrestling ever since he was very young, I always noticed that Kevin never seemed to learn the fine points that would make the difference in the higher levels of the sport. Still, he was successful and placed 3rd in the Nassau County Qualifying Tournament as a freshman—earning his first of 8 varsity letters in the three sports at the age of 14.

It was in lacrosse, however, where he truly excelled. Kevin and two other players were brought up to varsity as freshmen and helped lead us to an outstanding season with an undefeated record in our conference. The other two freshmen who were brought up were also quite talented athletes, high quality students, and outstanding young men of great personal character. I loved having Kevin in their company. We had an exceptional crop of athletes in Kevin's class, as well as the two grades that straddled his. There was great anticipation by the coaches that we were going to have some of our greatest success in football, wrestling, and lacrosse on the varsity level when these kids matured.

****

Chapter 5 –
Party for Lunch

While many high schools on Long Island have a closed campus (i.e. students may not leave the building area during lunch or a free period), Sherwood had no such restrictions. With 40-minute periods and 4 minutes between each class, the kids could go home or into the village close by for a bite to eat. It was in the winter of Kevin's junior year that this freedom began to be used for something other than food and innocent socialization. Some of Kevin's friends had discovered the excitement of smoking marijuana and would go to one of their houses for just that purpose.

Kevin had heard that his father and mother had both smoked their share of pot when they were younger, so he had not been scared away by any horror stories about the inherent evils of "partying". From the first time Kevin tried pot at age 16, he became an everyday user. As he was to later explain, the first several times he smoked pot he felt all the anxiety in him was released. He felt euphoric. He laughed, relaxed, and felt a strong camaraderie with those around him. At this stage he also probably felt that being the goody two shoes "coach's son" was a label he would choose to rebel against. He would much rather be cool among his peers than be the ideal student athlete in a parent's or teacher's eyes. And without question, he loved the "buzz" that smoking pot provided.

Marijuana was easy to get in high school. Older brothers of his friends were doing it and it was available for a small percentage of your lunch money. It only takes a few hits of a joint or pipe to get high and after the first 15 or 20 minutes or so, the high mellows out enough so that students can function in school generally undetected by teachers and administrators. The crowd that does party at lunch forms a social bond and they take some pride in being wild and cool. Returning to the classroom becomes more fun with the buzz you're experiencing than it otherwise would have. After a few hours, the high will have worn off in time to go practice on the athletic fields. There is no hangover. In Kevin's mind and those of this group of friends, this was a good way to go through their school day.

I can't say how many athletes of mine were in this condition but it is fair to say that some of my best were. One might ask, "How did this go undetected?" It is a tough question to answer but the best I can do is to say that high school kids act whacky on a normal day. It is tough to know if a kid is high or not and most teachers are focused on their lesson or curriculum instead of looking for bloodshot eyes or confused thinking. Even if a teacher did suspect a student of being high, challenging one without concrete proof could cause a problem. Parents were more likely to be in denial and would resent the teacher who challenged their son or daughter without presenting any solid evidence. If the teacher were wrong, it could be a nightmare.

In Kevin's case, there were colleagues of mine who were concerned about the company he was seen in and the change of attitude they witnessed in him. My belief was that Kevin was getting older and his rebellion of being the son of a high profile teacher and coach in the building was understandable. Even though I suspected that Kevin had tried smoking pot, I certainly had no idea it was a regular habit that took place during the school day.

There were signs, however. A cigarette lighter was found in his jeans pocket by Nanny on more than one occasion. His grades slipped a bit but nothing drastic. He was taking tougher courses and this was to be expected to some extent. He remained in denial at all times about smoking pot and even though I believed he was lying, I never imagined the frequency. Was I too lax on the investigation of this problem? As the situation turned out, yes, absolutely. Did I realize that Kevin was prone to a disease that would lead to use of harder drugs? No, but maybe I should have. As it unfolded over the years, my lax attitude toward marijuana would be a mistake. Could I have prevented his eventual descent into heroin addiction had I been more vigilant and nipped it in the bud at age 16? I will never know.

Chapter 6 –
Thoughts on Drinking and Drugging

No respectable father expects his son to ever become a heroin addict. Many responsible parents worry about drug use by their children. Because of this, it makes sense that if they had used drugs in their youth, they might lie or greatly diminish the amount of drinking and drugging that they participated in when speaking to their kids. This might very well be considered the responsible thing to do in order to discourage their children from doing the same thing.

Guys of my generation know something about drugs. I had plenty of experience drinking and smoking pot from my days in college and beyond. I worked as a bartender on weekends and summers for 18 years. Partying was a part of my life and I preferred the crowd that enjoyed this lifestyle. The 1970's and 80's were certainly years of many wild parties and Kevin's mom, CB, and I were certainly right in the middle of it all.

Although I can't really say I was ashamed of my behavior, I knew I had to hide it from my school community. My home and my bars were away from Sherwood and there could never be any mention of unprofessional behavior around the school community. I knew that I was a role model for my students and players. I kept my private life just that—private. I liked who I was, had little or no remorse for my lifestyle, and felt like a responsible citizen and important figure in the community. I was, however, careful to protect my reputation in Sherwood.

Unfortunately, I decided to be pretty open about it when talking to my sons about drug use. I felt that if I was going to convince my boys about the real dangers involved, I needed them to believe I was both truthful and knowledgeable. I believed that cocaine was incredibly dangerous and told them some of the horror stories associated with what was often called "The Big Lie." Cocaine and its derivatives was something to stay away from. It will severely hurt your health, bankrupt your personal finances, and never satisfy you for any period of time.

Marijuana, in my mind, was not a dangerous drug—at least not as dangerous as alcohol! Having tended bar for all those years, I knew all too well the many problems associated with alcohol. My belief was that kids from Long Island were eventually going to try both drinking and smoking pot, so it was better to be up front and honest about it with my sons. In speaking to them about marijuana, I spoke about "burn-outs" who had no ambition, no sense of responsibility. They cracked up cars, flunked out of college, couldn't hold a job, and never amounted to anything. But I admitted that I had smoked it back in the day.

Alcohol, however, is part of the fabric of American life and I never believed I could ever give them a healthy education about responsible drinking if I lied to them. Stories about drunks involving car accidents, excessive violence, destruction of property and significant illness seemed so much more prevalent than it did for potheads. My sons had always seen me, my family, and our friends drink at virtually every family party and holiday—just like we watched our parents do growing up. Because there was a deep history of alcoholism and drug addiction in our family, I certainly was being very cavalier about the possibilities that this disease would ever touch my children. I had, unfortunately dismissed the theory that marijuana was a gateway to more dangerous illegal drugs. Was I being irresponsible?

****

My father believed that his two sons never got in big trouble because they were brought up right. I think he was just lucky. As kids, Mike and I had enormous freedom. We could come and go as we pleased without strict curfews or restrictions. Drinking was a big part of the social life of what I call the World War II generation; so many of their funniest stories were about being drunk and the crazy things they did under the influence. We weren't exposed to the horrors of alcoholism. My parents and their friends went to work and raised their families while virtually drinking every day and night.

My dad, Marshall, probably drank close to a quart of liquor a day for more than 40 years. He was a loving dad, husband, and good friend to many. He was an excellent provider, a successful businessman, and a very funny and beloved character in the local bars. He dressed in fine suits, drove new cars, and we lived in an impressive house. Marsh had been a quality athlete in high school and had achieved the rank of major in the U.S. Army during World War II. He was the executive vice president of a successful printing supply company and received a healthy salary. In most every way my dad was considered an impressive man.

My mom drank much less than my dad, but they had cocktails together at the kitchen table every evening and often went out to bars and restaurants to drink with friends. It was said that my mom was like the TV moms on shows like "Leave it to Beaver" or "Father Knows Best." She was beautiful, well dressed, well mannered, very loving, and extremely efficient. When she drank, she was always the most fun of anyone in the room. My best friend, Stevie T, used to say that Phyllie presented herself like the wife of a foreign ambassador. She had class!

There was nothing in my life growing up that indicated that there was any great danger associated with being a big drinker. My parents and their friends raised strong families, remained loyal to their spouses, and had a great deal of fun together. It always involved drinking and it was never hidden from the children. We associated drinking with having fun, well before we ever started drinking ourselves.

My brother and I both started drinking around the age of 15, although the legal age was then 18. My friends and I would buy beers and drink together over the weekend in an empty lot hidden by trees.

I wasn't introduced to marijuana until college, but pot smoking was all over the high school scene by the time I started teaching a few years later in 1972. Smoking pot and drinking seemed to be a part of growing up on Long Island in the 1970's. Since my friends and I all turned out pretty well, I had little doubt that my boys would survive the world of partying like so many others did.

Chapter 7 –
No Down Side

Certainly the greatest motivation that I had for choosing Sherwood as the place to move when CB and I split was so Kevin could play for Sherwood and I could coach him. One great advantage was that I would be able to continue coaching without missing any of my son's games. Since my older boy, Matt, had played at the same time that I was coaching, I missed so many of his games. Matt seemed okay with it, but I never really was.

I had kept a careful eye on other coaches who had a son play for them. Many of the situations turned out successful but there was always a great risk. Parents and players could both believe that a coach favored his own son to the detriment of another kid on the team. There was bound to be gossip in the community about almost anything concerning the relationship between the coach and his son. There was automatic pressure for the coach to be totally unbiased and the player to be a model of sportsmanship and dedication.

Kevin and I were both willing to take the good with the bad—and there was a lot of good. Our record together consisted of a lot of wins and very few losses. The only New York State Championships in any team sport in Sherwood High School history took place in 1999 and 2000 in lacrosse. It was Kevin's junior and senior years and the Sherwood community was on fire over our success. Big signs were put up on Sunrise Highway declaring Sherwood as the "Home of the State Champs" and every player had a big sign placed in front of his house announcing that "A NY State Champion Lives Here."

Local politicians flocked to us to have our pictures taken together. Signs, banners, and pictures adorned the windows of local stores and businesses and we were greeted with warmth and affection all over town.

Kevin received All County honors in both his junior and senior seasons and set offensive records for the most assists in Sherwood history—a record that still stands 10 years later. He was nominated for All-American in his senior year and received Honorable Mention recognition. We had some great players in those years and Kevin was certainly one of them. He received several scholarship offers from some of the top colleges in the country and accepted one from the Northern University in Massachusetts. We were thrilled because Northern was coached by Greg Randazzo, a former Sherwood lacrosse star.

As the coach, I was inducted into the Long Island—Metropolitan Lacrosse Hall of Fame as a crowning achievement of my long career up to that time after our first State Championship in '99. Kevin and I received a lot of attention in local newspapers and on local TV. There were many team parties, awards dinners, and assemblies that we attended together. We received congratulatory phone calls, emails, and letters from people from all different stages of our lives. It was a magical time for us both, for our family and all the other families involved.

When Kevin graduated Sherwood HS in 2000, our decision to move to town 7 years earlier appeared to have been a brilliant maneuver with really no down side. And the future looked equally bright.

Chapter 8 –
Big Life Changes

When Kevin left for Northern University many things changed for our family. First of all, Phyllie seemed to have lost her function. Without Kevin around, she believed that she had little purpose left in life. She also knew that I had become serious with my girlfriend of about 3 years, Laura, and, although this made her happy for me, I no longer wanted her to take care of me either. I wanted to live with Laura, not live alone with my mom. Our house in Sherwood, however, was not really well set up to move Laura in with us. Phyllie had the master bedroom and the apartment downstairs was really better suited for a single guy. Laura loved the beach and was renting in Long Beach, a beautiful city on the Atlantic Ocean only an easy 17 minute ride from Sherwood. Now that Kevin was out of high school, I wanted to buy a place with Laura as close to the ocean as we could arrange.

We asked Phyllie if she would look for a house with us that would be set up so she, Laura and I could have privacy but still live together with her. I didn't want my mom to be alone, and Laura and Phyllie got along great. At first she reluctantly assented to the arrangement. But after looking at houses together, Phyllie decided that she had no interest in living in Long Beach and would prefer to live in a small apartment on her own. Laura and I tried to talk her out of this idea, but she became more adamant about wanting to be on her own. My brother, Mike, convinced me that Phyllie really didn't want to move in with Laura and me, so we looked for a nice apartment for Phyllie to rent. I didn't feel great about this arrangement, particularly because Phyllie seemed to be failing a bit mentally at age 80, and she often spoke fearfully about "losing her mind." Her mom, my grandma Maud, had suffered from dementia in her 80's and now Phyllie became almost obsessed with this fear that it was going to happen to her.

Phyllie was a caring, loving mom all my life. I know she wanted me to be happy and to be able to start a new life together with Laura. She believed that she would be a burden on the new relationship if she was in the same house. She also valued her independence above all else. Laura and I both tried to convince her that it would be better if we all lived together. Yet by the summer of 2001, Phyllie had moved into a nice one bedroom apartment nearby, our house had been sold, and I moved into Laura's apartment temporarily until we could find a bigger and better place for us in Long Beach. Kevin moved back into his old room in Merrick with his mom and his brother, Matt.

Although this big move led to my marriage to Laura within a year and great personal happiness for us both, it was the beginning of a downward spiral for both Phyllie and Kevin. Looking back, I can't say that anything we did then was the cause of Phyllie's steep decline or Kevin's descent into drug addiction but they took place simultaneously. Phyllie soon developed severe pain in her hip that led to a hip replacement. The general anesthesia from that operation had a bad effect on her mental faculties, from which she never fully recovered.

Whether it was dementia or Alzheimer's disease, I don't know, but it was progressive and she was never the same. She was terribly fearful about losing her mind. It seemed the more she thought about it, the worse it got, a self-fulfilling prophecy. Nevertheless, Phyllie's personality changed drastically. For the last five years of her life, she seemed always afraid and became self-centered for the first time in her life. The rock of our family who had taken care of us from birth to adulthood now needed our constant attention. And it was difficult to make her happy because she was always afraid. It is a horrible disease

When later Phyllie died of a sudden heart attack in 2006, she was released of all her fear and anxiety. It was a merciful ending for a fabulous woman. She was, however, spared from ever knowing that her cherished grandson, Kevin, had become the family nightmare.

Chapter 9 –
Bad Signs

I thought college was the ideal life for me back in the late 60's and early 70's. Kevin, however, didn't enjoy college as much as I did. He seemed to often get a ride home on weekends to see his friends. NU was a three and a half hour ride and Kevin seemed a little homesick. He earned solid grades in his first year and received some important playing time as a freshman attackman on the NU varsity lacrosse team. There was really little reason to suspect that Kevin was about to fall into the downward spiral of addiction. Nevertheless, he already was an addict of marijuana. A pot addiction is not easily detectable and allows one to function without overt signs of an imminent problem.

By the summer of 2001, I had moved into Long Beach with Laura. Kevin moved back into the Merrick house with his mom and brother. I got Kevin a 1995 Nissan Altima so he could come and go to college on his own. Although the car was a gift, he was told that he would need to get a part time job at school in order to pay for expenses like gas and repairs. I didn't realize at the time one of the biggest expenses would be his numerous parking tickets.

Lacrosse is a sport played in the spring season and I realized that it would be difficult to play, go to school, and hold a part time job. I encouraged him to get a job for the fall and winter to earn enough to help pay his car expenses. I sent him an allowance for food and minor expenses. He had a meal plan card he could use on campus and at many local stores and restaurants in the town. I set him up with a bank account that I could put money into and he could withdraw with a bank card that worked as a debit card.

The signs of a problem began to show up with this bank account during his sophomore year. Because Kevin's mom and I were divorced, Kevin could get his mom to send him money complaining to her that I was tight with his allowance. He started to lie to both of us about how much money he needed and was receiving from us. When CB told me the amount of cash she was doling out to him each week, I was astounded. No matter how much money I put into that account, it disappeared just that quickly. He also never got a part time job, complaining of his difficult course load and the demanding conditioning programs run throughout the school year by the lacrosse team. Most obvious was that he was lying and throwing temper tantrums of constant denials when either his mother or I would point out the discrepancies in his stories. He also returned home to Long Island often on the weekends without my knowing it.

The obvious question was, "Where was the money going?" It was a question for which he never had a good answer. Suspicion of drug use did occur to me, certainly. I had a personal relationship with Kevin's lacrosse coach, Greg Randazzo, who was a former great player of mine at Sherwood in the early 80's. My trust in him was a chief reason that we chose Northern University over other scholarship offers for Kevin.

Although Greg didn't have any definitive answers for me, he was open to the possibility that something was wrong. Greg was a tough coach and was, perhaps, particularly tough on Kevin—wanting to get the best from him. Kevin complained about the coach now being unfairly tough on him in the off-season morning workouts. It seemed that Kevin wasn't taking responsibility for anything that was going wrong. When he got caught in a lie, he would continue to deny it anyway. He projected blame on to me, his mother, his coach, his teachers, the school, the campus police, etc. And the grades started to slip, courses started to get dropped, and his performance on the lacrosse field was not really up to his potential.

****

The most telling sign came during the winter of his sophomore year when I realized that a $960 refund check for health insurance that I was expecting from the college had not arrived. I had overpaid the college for their health plan that Kevin didn't need and was guaranteed by the NU health officials that the money would be returned. When more than a month had gone by, I called the health insurance office at NU and found out that the check had been sent to Kevin Glenz four weeks earlier. Colleges deal with the student, not the parent when it comes to finances, even though it is the parent who pays. That check for $960 had Kevin's name on it.

The phone conversation was not one of the highlights of my life as a loving father. I asked Kevin, "Did you get a check for $960 a month ago from the college?" He didn't seem to understand the question, saying, "What are you talking about?" I explained the whole health care insurance refund situation and asked him the same question again. This time he said, "I remember getting something but I don't think it was for that much. I think it was for a couple of hundred or something." As I felt the blood rushing to my head, I realized that I was ready to explode into an uncontrollable rage and I needed to calm down before I continued the conversation. After taking a minute to try to collect myself, Kevin continued, "Anyway, it had my name on it." The conversation continued something like this with each reply increasing in volume and aggressiveness in tone.

Dad: Where is the money now?

Kevin: What do you mean?

Dad: What do you think I mean. Where's the fucking $960 now.

Kevin: It wasn't $960 and anyway it had my name on it.

Dad: I guarantee you it was $960, you lying piece of shit? Now I'm going to ask you again, where is the fucking money?

Kevin: Where is it? I don't know. I spent it, I guess. I'm sure it wasn't that much. Hey look, that check had my name on it. When I get a check with my name on it, I figure it's mine. I owed a few guys some money that I paid back. I paid some of my parking tickets (lie). I had to pay some stuff for my car (lie). I didn't ask mom for any money that month. I don't know; the money goes. Anyway, it was less money than you said and it had my name on it.

Dad: How much do you have left?

Kevin: What do you mean? It was a month ago, I don't have any left. Anyway, it had my name on it so I thought it was mine. Why didn't you say something sooner if you wanted it?

I'm glad now that there were 230 miles between the two of us at that moment. I called him every derogatory name I could think of. I threatened to beat his skinny ass to death when I saw him. I threatened to take him out of college, take back his car, and continued to call him the foulest things that came to mind. It would be one of several more times to come where I would completely lose my cool and behave as a violent lunatic.

Kevin had become and would remain my greatest teacher. I would learn a great deal about myself from Kevin's drug addiction. Not all learning is fun.

Chapter 10 –
Religion and Spirituality

Until my separation from my first wife, CB, most of my life had been bereft of spirituality. No one who ever knew me before my mid-forties could have possibly considered me a candidate for becoming an Ordained Ministerial Counselor (O.M.C.) or what is more commonly referred to as a Reverend. Without a strong spiritual path, however, I would have never been able to handle Kevin's addiction without making my life and the life of those around me completely miserable. Even with an increasing connection to my Higher Power, I screwed up plenty. But Kevin's addiction would serve as a classroom for me to learn the power of forgiveness.

From the time I was confirmed as a Presbyterian at age 13, I quickly lost any conscious contact with a God of my understanding. When I hit college age, I was developing a strong agnostic philosophy. As a history major in college and then as a high school history teacher starting at age 22, I realized that the organized religions seemed to have a really bad historical record as far as love, compassion, and human understanding is concerned. I didn't necessarily accept the concept of God as pure superstition as atheists do, but the use of religion as a method of social control throughout history was painfully apparent.

World history is full of horrible violence between religious sects all claiming to be followers of a "Prince of Peace." As a student and teacher of Global Studies, I was familiar with the fundamental beliefs of Judaism, Christianity, Islam, Buddhism, Hinduism, Taoism, Shinto,

Zoroastrianism, and some of the basic differences that exist within the many denominations of a particular religion. The endless warfare, massacre, torture, occupation, genocide, that is both history and current events completely turned me off to religious moral authority.

All of these violent actions seemed to be the antithesis of their core teachings of love, compassion, and forgiveness. Catholics and Protestants butchered each other throughout Europe for over a millennium. The Islamic empires that conquered parts of Asia, Africa, and Europe were accomplished through "jihad" or holy war against non-believers. The Crusades violated all the loving teachings of Jesus. Even in my lifetime, Protestants and Catholics terrorized each other in Ireland, Jews and Muslims slaughtered each other in the Mideast, as have Hindus and Muslims on the Indian subcontinent. The list of organized religions involved in mass killing in the name of God is truly endless.

It seemed so obvious to me that organized religions divided us. But within the organized religions are sincere people trying to connect to their Higher Power, their Inner Guidance, the Universal Spirit in us. There is a **knowing** within each of us that can sense there is something so much greater than ourselves to which we are connected. Organized religions have historically exploited that **knowing** and divided us from each other while claiming unique knowledge of God's plan. Those who disagreed were called heretics or infidels and subjected to banishment, torture, and execution.

I believe mankind will always yearn for his connection to his Creator to be revealed to him. My father always said, "There are no atheists in foxholes." It does appear that fear is a great motivator in one's decision to turn to God. Historically, organized religions have exploited that fear.

Nevertheless, one's true connection to his Higher Power is the greatest inner strength one can possess. It is with a strong connection to Spirit that alcoholics and drug addicts have been able to overcome the ravages of their disease. This is why nothing except a devotion to the Twelve Steps of Alcoholics Anonymous has enabled so many millions of alcoholics/addicts to defeat their demons. The Twelve Steps is a spiritual path of the highest order.

Chapter 11 –
A Major Change in My Life

———⋙•◇•⋘———

Despite my long adherence to an agnostic philosophy, something deep inside wanted to connect with the eternal. It was my separation from my wife CB that opened the door to a spiritual connection. When after 19 years of marriage, my wife told me she was no longer in love with me, it shook my whole world. My friend, Murf, was going through the same thing with his wife at the same time. We both had two kids and we did not understand then what had happened to our marriages. As friends do, we relied on each other for support. When I made plans to move to Sherwood with my mom and Kevin, Murf offered to rent our basement apartment if we were willing. It was a good financial move for us, but it proved to be so much more significant than that.

While Murf was trying to deal with the emptiness that comes from divorce, a business friend handed him a book on tape that he said had helped him overcome a bout with testicular cancer. Murf had listened to it, liked it, and asked me if I wanted to try it out. I figured I had nothing to lose so I took the tape. I had never had a book on tape before and I had never heard of the book, *A Return to Love,* or its author, Marianne Williamson. Murf said he and his friend had found it "inspiring" and I figured, the way I was feeling, I could use some inspiration. My car had a tape deck and I could listen to it there.

The author and voice on the tape was a woman who had a message of self help in handling life's difficulties by following a self study course of spiritual psychotherapy called *A Course in Miracles*. She talked about forgiveness of others and yourself. The philosophy that Marianne Williamson was describing called for a person to never consider himself or herself to be a victim of anyone or anything. She said we create everything that happens to us and we receive what we ask for. We are in control of our thoughts and these thoughts determine what happens in our life. Although these were new and different concepts to me, I was intrigued and she seemed to apply it all to situations to which I could identify (e.g. relationships, romance, careers, money, and prestige).

I listened to this tape over and over again. I would keep driving or just pull over somewhere alone in my car so I could continue to listen to her voice. I would put it in my Walkman and take long walks or sit or lie down with it. For a while, listening to this tape was all I wanted to do.

There were many references to the Holy Spirit, Jesus, and God. *A Course in Miracles* is a three volume set that claims to be authored by Jesus through a scribe. I loved Marianne Williamson's voice and the things she said for the most part were attractive to me. But having been an agnostic for 30 years, there was a lot to which I was resistant.

When Murf asked me how I liked the tape, I responded, "I love it. I listen to it over and over again. I can hardly stay away from it." He said, "That's great. So it really is doing something for you, huh?" I said, "Definitely." But then I asked, "Do you think I could do this *A Course in Miracles* without all this God shit, though. You know I'm not into the God shit." Murf paused, thought a little bit, and replied, "I really don't know." Murf always possessed an understated sense of wisdom.

I asked him if his friend had anything else from Marianne Williamson. He said that he actually had lots of material from lectures that she did all over the country. When I received several more tapes, I immersed myself in this woman's lectures and became more and more intrigued by the philosophy itself that so inspired her. She spoke of the Workbook of *A Course in Miracles* and the daily lessons it provided. She said you didn't have to believe the lessons or agree with them. You didn't even have to like them. She said it was "like lifting weights." If you devote yourself to the lesson every day, you will be spiritually strengthened.

Murf and I found out when Marianne was coming to lecture in New York City. Murf worked in the city so I took the train in to meet him. The tickets were only $10 and I remember that the people who couldn't afford it could go free. The building was called *Town Hall* and it was an old, classic styled theater off Broadway. When Murf and I walked in it was hard to miss the fact that there were about five times as many women as men. Both of us had not had a girlfriend since our breakups, so we were immediately attracted to the fine assortment of beautiful females surrounding us. Neither one of us had much of a pick-up line, however. Not only were we out of practice, we weren't very smooth with the ladies anyway. Nevertheless, we both had trouble thinking of anything else until the keynote speaker arrived.

Marianne Williamson is also a fabulous looking woman and *soooo* cool. I felt like I fell in love with her the second I saw her and my passion only increased as she spoke. She has an engaging personality and a somewhat earthy sense of humor that only made me more enamored. She spoke a good deal about romantic relationships among many topics. I remember her saying to people in the audience, "Have you yet become the kind of person that you would like to have as a partner? Because that's what you have to work on first. You don't need anyone else to make you complete. You need to strengthen your own connection to your own Inner Guidance. The Universe will take care of the rest of the details."

There was a long question and answer session with the audience at the end of her lecture. It became apparent that many of these beautiful people were as spiritually starved as I was. On the way out of the theater, there was a huge book and tape sale. I picked up a few more tapes of hers and the three book set of *A Course of Miracles*—the Text, the Workbook, and the Manual for Teachers.

As we walked the streets of Manhattan after the lecture, we came upon a famed "gentlemen's club" called *Runway 69* in midtown Manhattan. We were two healthy men who had been sexually starved for quite a while and entertainment like this held more than a casual interest. We stopped at the door with the plastic bag of the three heavy books of *A Course in Miracles*. We looked at each other, paused for a few moments and quietly said simultaneously, "Naaaaah!" while shaking our heads. We just didn't want these spiritual books in this bawdy establishment, so we blew off the strip club and wound up going to a more traditional bar and talked about the concepts of *A Course in Miracles* that we had just listened to in Marianne Williamson's lecture.

Somehow we knew that these books were going to be of enormous value in our lives and we wanted them to be accorded the proper respect. After a few beers, we caught the train to Sherwood and I started reading Lesson 1 in the Workbook on the ride home. This was the beginning of a major change in my life and one that would give me the inner strength to deal with all that was to come with Kevin.

Chapter 12 –
Quitters Never Win

In February of Kevin's junior year, another sign that something was wrong emerged. Kevin called and said he was quitting the lacrosse team, quitting school and coming home. Apparently the NU team had not played well against Dartmouth in a pre-season scrimmage on a brutally cold field and Coach Randazzo decided to shake up things to get the team playing better before next week's season opener. He called Kevin into his office and said in no uncertain terms that he was not getting enough production out of Kevin and some of his teammates on the offense. As a result, he was changing Kevin's position from attack to midfield and challenged him to make a contribution in a new role.

Although the coach has every right to organize his team in any way that he feels will help them be most successful, Kevin perceived it as a personal attack. In Kevin's mind, Coach Randazzo was blaming the team's lack of offensive production on him. Since Kevin had never played the position of midfield, he saw this as a demotion.

No player wants to hear news like this, but Kevin reacted terribly. Convinced that the coach didn't like him and that he was being unfairly blamed for the team's lack of offensive production, Kevin cut off the meeting before it was over and stormed out in a fury. He immediately made a decision to quit the team—something he had never done before and a decision that I would find impossible to support. As a player and a coach, I have always believed and taught that quitting is a coward's way out. Nothing good can come from quitting. Every good athlete and coach believes the clichés, "When the going gets tough, the tough get going." "Quitters never win and winners never quit."

Kevin had always been sensitive to criticism and would get defensive whenever a coach would ride him with some negative, tough guy rhetoric. But this was an almost absurd overreaction. He had not been jettisoned from the team's plans but was redeployed under a new plan. He never could be convinced of this and decided to walk away from it all—a victim of gross unfairness by a tyrannical overseer.

It is unlikely that a player can walk away from a coach in the middle of a one on one meeting—miss practice by going home under those circumstances, and still retain his scholarship and position on the team. Kevin knew that, but he was overwhelmed by his perception that he had unfairly lost his job and that the situation was irrevocable. "Where was his mental toughness," I wondered? "Didn't he have enough guts to hang in there and prove to the coach he could be a great asset to the team? Why was he being so soft and temperamental? He was playing in Division 1 now, for Christ sake! Suck it up and prove the coach wrong. Never, ever quit!"

My entire life was filled with these axioms of athletic coaching. Hadn't he been brought up to face these types of challenges? I was feeling sick to my stomach and deeply depressed. Once he walks away, there can be no going back.

It was the experience of being in this emotional pain as Kevin's father that led me to turn to the Holy Spirit as I had been taught by *A Course in Miracles*. In my spiritual search to find my connection to the Holy Spirit, I found a process of contemplation that allowed me to hand over my problems to my Higher Power in order to receive the wisest advice.

The following is my contemplation from my journal on February 17, 2003. It would be just one of many times that I would use this process to connect to my Higher Power.

Question: *Kevin has called to say he quit the lacrosse team and is leaving NU. How do I best react to help Kevin?*

My Thoughts: *Kevin has always had a bad attitude when criticized, and his battles with Randazzo are consistent. He doesn't do what he is told and rejects authority in general. By cutting off the meeting with the coach, he's demonstrated that he is not willing to compromise or cooperate. Randazzo is probably (certainly) fed up with him. He obviously is not playing great and the coach needs to make a move. By telling Kevin to switch to midfield, he is offering Kevin a playing opportunity but a demotion. Kevin hates Randazzo right now and is miserable. He wants to quit school too, because attending school without playing lacrosse is unacceptable. Quitting goes against everything I've ever believed—but I know those beliefs don't work for Kevin. It hurts me to let him quit—but support for Kevin right now is probably the smart move for him and our relationship.*

> **Pray for Grace (1 minute) followed by meditation (5-10 minutes):**
> **Answer: Let him go—Kevin has a lot of growing up to do. There truly is no other choice. He won't stay even if you demanded it. Kevin hates lacrosse now. That should settle it. Lacrosse is supposed to be played with joy. There hasn't been joy in it for him in a while. This will teach him more than anything else could have. There is no other choice—if he wants to leave, let him go. Do everything possible to remove guilt or shame from him or yourself. Nothing is going to be smooth with Kevin. Love him anyway.**

****

When I met with Kevin the next day in my condo in Long Beach, he was distraught. I asked my old college friend, Carl, if he would meet with us as sort of a buffer. Carl was also a high school football and wrestling coach and had known Kevin since birth. Carl's presence was remarkable in helping to make this a calm and loving situation. Kevin liked Carl and sensed that he would be a calming influence in this difficult father-son discussion.

Kevin explained the situation as he saw it. He could not imagine playing the position of midfield and didn't believe he could be of any help to the team. He recognized that walking out on the meeting was unacceptable but said he felt like leaping across the desk and pummeling the coach with punches—so he believed leaving the scene to be preferable. I tried to make Kevin comfortable telling his side of the story by saying, "I can understand how you could feel that way." He believed, as did I, that the coach would never take him back after this scene that had occurred.

Carl asked Kevin a few questions. "Do you still want to play, if you could get back on the team?" Kevin answered, "Yes, but I don't think he would take me back now." Carl asked, "Would you be willing to call him to find out?" Kevin was obviously ashamed to call his coach and did not want to take the chance of being rebuked. Kevin didn't know I had already talked to Coach Randazzo. Greg felt badly about Kevin's reaction and the idea of losing him was a no-win situation for everyone. The coach definitely wanted him back, but I didn't want to tell that to Kevin.

I offered to call Coach Randazzo with Kevin next to me. He quickly assented to that arrangement and when I got the coach on the phone, he asked to speak to Kevin. I didn't hear what Greg said to Kevin, but when it was over, Kevin had a look of relief on his face and tears in his eyes. "I can't believe it. He really wants me back." Kevin said as a smile emerged through the tears. We all hugged each other and Kevin said, "I've got to get right back to school before I miss another practice." Carl and I patted Kevin on the back, wished him luck, and told him to make us all proud. Kevin rushed away feeling like a death sentence had been lifted.

When I had talked to Carl the night before, we both believed that there was a possibility of a drug problem causing this whole scenario. I asked Carl what he thought about that now. From what he had just experienced, he didn't believe that was the problem. At that moment, neither did I—but we were wrong. Kevin had already started to experiment with snorting Oxycontin. This reprieve from quitting lacrosse would hold the wolf at bay—but only temporarily.

Chapter 13 –
Ask and Listen

Kevin returned to NU and the lacrosse team after his blow out meeting with the coach in February. Coach Randazzo decided not to change Kevin's position but did successfully shuffle the offensive players into a highly potent scoring machine. The NU team had an outstanding season winning the ECAC (East Coast Athletic Conference) Championship and earning a berth in the NCAA Division I Tournament—winning the first playoff game before losing to the University of Maryland in the quarterfinals at the Dome in Syracuse. Kevin played a prominent role in his team's success and was certainly in a position to be one of the senior leaders, if not a captain, the following year.

Laura and I loved going to the games. We were thrilled to have Kevin playing well and enjoyed visiting schools like the University of North Carolina, Georgetown University, Brown, Yale, and Princeton. Our joy was tempered by our suspicion that something was wrong and our guess was that drugs were involved. Kevin had dropped a few classes and his behavior was erratic. We had not yet learned of his use of Oxycontin, a highly addictive opiate. The wheels had not yet fallen off and we had no solid evidence. Kevin returned to Merrick to live with his mom and avoided me as much as possible.

My time schedule for Kevin to straighten out his act appeared to be a lot different than Holy Spirit's. I wanted him fixed immediately, and yet, I still didn't fully know the problem. My fears about Kevin did help me to connect to my Higher Power more and more often. I felt helpless on my own and *A Course in Miracles* had taught me to turn all my concerns and problems to the Holy Spirit, Inner Guidance, Higher Self, or any name with which I felt comfortable.

On page 70 of ACIM's *Manual for Teachers*, it refers to the Holy Spirit's function in helping.

> **"Ask and He will answer. The responsibility is His, and He alone is fit to assume it. To do so is His function. To refer the questions to Him is yours. Would you want to be responsible for decisions about which you understand so little? His answers are always right. Would you say that about yours?"**

This is my contemplation with Holy Spirit from July 9, 2003.

Question: How can I help Kevin with his college and career choices when he shows so little initiative?

My Thoughts: I found out today that Kevin will not graduate NU with a teaching degree. He has shown so little initiative. He has no place to stay in the fall. He has not checked out what is necessary to graduate. He is now a sociology major with no idea what that actually is. It just seems worthless to me. He will not graduate on time and will have no scholarship after this year. He seems so helpless—he won't do anything on his own. He's barely working at all this summer. He has little contact with me and is avoiding coming to see me. I know I should back off but then nothing will get done. Laura has been great through this, but she just can't believe this kid. I so much want to take the correct action or non-action.

> ***Pray for Grace followed by meditation:***
> ***Answer: Most important, don't get angry with Kevin or show your disappointment. Lay out the choices for him as you understand them—again, without judgment and, particularly, without anger or disgust. Kevin will always***

*be different than what you want. Allow him to be. It's his
life to make mistakes and experience the consequences.
When he comes to you for genuine advice and help, do
whatever feels right. It is impossible to predict Kevin's
future.*

****

I've learned that praying to Holy Spirit and following His advice
are two different things. My tendency was to ask Him for advice and
then do what my ego felt was right. I was upset that Kevin was no
longer on track to become a teacher. I continued to get angry, show
disgust, and point out what a "piece of shit" this kid had become.

ACIM teaches me that if I screw up my opportunities for
forgiveness, I will feel anger, fear and anxiety. But I will get another
opportunity soon to do it right. I screwed up a lot. It takes a lot of
practice turning things over to your Inner Guidance before you're
really ready to listen. But there is a lot of anger, frustration and fear
in following my own guidance instead of Holy Spirit's.

Chapter 14 –
Whitefish, MT.

L aura and I took an amazing trip to the northern Rocky Mountains for two weeks in the summer of 2003. We flew into Jackson Hole, WY and rented a car. For two weeks we traveled north through this incredible countryside, stopping for days in the Grand Teton, Yellowstone, and Glacier National Parks—then heading up to Banff and Jasper in Alberta, Canada.

We met a lot of people during our trip but two people made a strong lasting impression concerning my relationship with Kevin. Laura and I met a big guy named Tim in a great looking restaurant / bar called *The Great Northern* in Whitefish, MT. Tim was in his mid-thirties and was having a few drinks at the bar with his mom, Alice. Like most people we met on our trip, Tim recognized that my accent was not from this area of the country and he struck up a conversation with the two of us. Alice was equally friendly and after talking about our trip for a while, the conversation turned to this mother-son relationship of Alice and Tim.

Tim was saying how he was such a hell raiser in his teens and 20's and how much trouble he got into in his youth. Alice smiled at some of Tim's recollections and winced at some others as Tim continued with tales of wildness and rebellion in high school, college, and after. They spoke about how the dad would try to talk some sense into his screwed up son and how frustrated Alice and her husband would get at being unable to get any cooperation out of Tim. They talked about how Tim paid some consequences for his actions, but still wasn't ready to listen to anyone about straightening out his act.

Tim now had a successful business, was engaged to be married, and had matured in his lifestyle and repaired his relationship with his family. Before Tim had struck up a conversation with us, Laura and I had been discussing Kevin and his aberrant behavior. We then mentioned to Tim and Alice that we were having our own problems with our rebellious kid who doesn't seem to be on the right track. We expressed how worried we were and how we feared that drugs might be involved.

Tim and Alice had a message for us that I don't think I'll ever forget. When they said this to us, I felt something inside of me light up as if I was being told something directly from the Holy Spirit. Tim said, "The seeds are already planted; it will take years until they mature." His reference was to the fact that I had instilled values into Kevin for many years—values that are deeply planted in him, even if they don't show now. His mom supported this by saying she had years of frustration with Tim. Tim said the values that his father had drilled into him were rejected earlier in his life but they never left him. They advised me to just hang in there.

Both of them seemed to be sent to me that night to give me an important message that Holy Spirit had been telling me in meditations but that I had trouble hearing. Kevin needs to experience whatever is his karma. From his experiences he will grow to understand what is really important and what really makes him happy. He will never forget my efforts to teach him solid values and will remember them and accept them as he matures.

I needed to hear that because I had lost confidence. Somehow I knew that those two people were sent to me. There are no accidents. The Holy Spirit had sent a couple of angels to me to prepare me for the heartache that was to unfold. I was being reminded that I had done my job as a father. That was all I could do.

When I returned to our motel outside of Glacier National Park on the Montana—Alberta border, I meditated on the experience with the mother—son couple in *The Great Northern*. I received the message clearly that I needed to remember. If Kevin comes to me for help or advice, give it; otherwise back away and let him learn from life's lessons, the way he is supposed to. The last part of the message advised me, **"Don't forget this."**

I picked up *A Course in Miracles* and went to the *Manual for Teachers.* In the section called "Clarification of Terms," I read the first paragraph of the Epilogue.

> *"Forget not once this journey is begun the end is certain. Doubt along the way will come and go and go to come again. Yet is the ending sure. No one can fail to do what God has appointed him to do. When you forget, remember that you walk with Him and with His Word upon your heart."*

Although my heart soared with confidence that I was in good hands as far as my efforts to help Kevin were concerned, I would forget to turn to my Inner Guidance when I was in the midst of the battle. I was, however, strengthening my belief in the power of connection to the Holy Spirit. I didn't know then of how serious Kevin's problem was, but I was being prepared to go the distance. It was going to be long and often ugly. I had the most powerful of allies with me if I could remember to walk with Him. No matter how the saga of Kevin turned out, with His help I would be strong enough to handle it.

Chapter 15 –
The Most Valuable Lesson
I Can Teach

It was in October that I found out that Kevin had pocketed $450 of the summer rent I had given him for his apartment at school. He lied about it numerous times but then changed his story and said he told me all about it and I just forgot. While catching him in this obvious lie, Kevin showed no remorse. Instead he continued his defense that he has been unfairly accused by a demanding, controlling, and vindictive father. His attacks on me focused on his statements that nothing he ever does will be good enough for me. My frustrations overwhelmed me and I decided to do a process of spiritual meditation to ask my Higher Power how I can best handle this.

The following are my notes from my contemplation from October 4, 2003:

Question: How do I handle the apparent dishonesty of my son, Kevin, and teach him proper values and lessons that will sustain him in the future?

My Thoughts: My natural instincts are to close down on all that is done. Take away his car—limit his money—make him get a job if he wants anything. Show him that there are consequences to his continuing dishonesty. The problem is that he can't function from where he lives at college without the car. Kevin cracks under any pressure. With no car, he won't go to class—he'll probably screw up school and lacrosse. In his mind, all this will be unfair. They'll be no lesson learned at this point; maybe after he grows up, he'll understand. But now, it just seems like a formula for disaster. He and I will have little contact. I won't feel right about his being on his own. Please direct me to be most loving while teaching Kevin what he needs to know.

> **Pray for Grace (1 minute) followed by Meditation:**
> **Answer: The most valuable lesson that you can teach Kevin now is that you have "unconditional love" for him. This love does not depend on whether or not he behaves according to your standards. He may be 21 but he has the maturity of a 16 year old. Shaming him won't work. Point out the actions that are inappropriate and explain why. Do so without showing anguish, disappointment, and disgust for his apparent lack of integrity. This is the time for you to be a great parent. Don't follow the old standards of discipline. Your spiritual practice now allows you a deeper understanding. By showing compassion in the face of his apparent betrayal—you're teaching a lesson of unconditional love—and he'll remember to do this with his own children. You've asked—I've answered— now follow this important advice—not what your gut reaction is telling you because you feel he has betrayed you.**

Chapter 16 –
A Coach with Integrity

I t was an email response from NU's lacrosse coach, Greg Randazzo, to my wife, Laura, which brought me to uncontrollable tears for the first time I can remember as an adult. It was a simple reply to Laura's inquiry about Kevin's condition in the fall of his senior year. Laura read the email to me. Greg said that he had no proof but he seriously suspected that there was a drug problem. When he said that, I knew he was talking about something more than smoking weed.

I went into my room and sat on the bed. Of course, it made sense but something had kept me in denial for at least the last six months. Kevin had turned into someone I really didn't know. We hated the sight of each other; we cringed at the sound of each other's voice on the phone. We treated each other with such an absence of respect that any extended time in each other's company could lead to physical violence. I couldn't tolerate his disrespect, his total ingratitude, his defiance, his dishonesty. He despised my sarcastic disapproval, my superior attitude, my condescending tone of voice, my look of disgust. Of course it made sense that he had a drug problem. I needed some independent confirmation; and now I felt I had received it from a trusted source, Coach Randazzo.

It seemed as if all the frustration from the last year had hit me all at one time. I started to cry so violently that I felt like passing out. My whole body shook with what felt like convulsions. What had happened to that wonderful little boy—the boy who wanted to be a great student athlete—the boy who adored his father and wanted to be just like him? Where was the overachieving super kid—the kid with the shining, bright blue eyes, asking a thousand questions—the kid who jumped on me to playfully wrestle me every time I was sitting comfortably? That kid was gone and another awful kid had slipped into his bigger body and possessed him. My crying kept on and felt like it wouldn't end. Laura had never seen me like this and it quite reasonably broke her heart. Needless to say, it was a bad night for both of us. I fell asleep from exhaustion, but when I awoke I spent hours asking the Holy Spirit's help to handle this with strength and compassion.

****

I called Greg Randazzo the next day. There were few people whom I trusted more. The coach's father, John, started lacrosse in Sherwood in 1957 as a physical education teacher. As a high school administrator, John could no longer coach but had a great passion for filling the coaching staff with the best people he could find. I am honored that he liked me from my interview and he was instrumental in my obtaining the job. In my first season as the freshman lacrosse coach in 1973 I coached John's oldest son, Michael. Greg was John's fifth and youngest son at age 7.

When I was appointed the head varsity lacrosse coach for Sherwood in 1982, Greg was a junior and an outstanding player. Although he was very talented, it was his attitude and toughness that distinguished him most from other players. When I needed to make decisions on team personnel or game strategies, it was a wise move to get Greg alone, one on one, to see what he thought. He was tremendously competitive and diligent but he also had a "game sense" that surpassed his coaches. I was glad I could recognize those remarkable traits in one of my players and by doing so, we formed a bond of trust. It turns out that that bond of trust would last much longer and become much more important than I could have ever known.

College coaches are in a different position than high school coaches in some ways. There is much more pressure to win on a college coach. Both are truly educators of young men but a high school coach is considered a teacher first who does an extracurricular activity after school for a small stipend. The job of a Division 1 college coach, like Greg Randazzo at NU, is 100% about coaching.

At the Northern University, we were fortunate enough to have a coach who was both a quality educator of young men and a field general who could produce a very competitive team. Kevin Glenz was lucky to have a coach who cared deeply about his well being and, as Kevin's father, I will be forever grateful.

Chapter 17 –
Ready to Help Kevin

Following Coach Randazzo's email to Laura, I became convinced that I had to do something about Kevin's alleged drug problem. I first needed to know if it was true. The most trusted source for me was my son, Matt. Matt loves Kevin but would not lie to me if he believed I was trying to help his brother. Matt knew from his mom that Kevin had been behaving crazily and she suspected drugs. After doing a little investigating, Matt told me that Kevin's problem was "pain killers." I knew nothing about them, but I knew I was ready to act. I turned to my Inner Guidance in the process of contemplation.

Question: *What can I do as a parent to find out what is going on with Kevin; what exactly is his problem and how can I help him?*

My Thoughts: *Talking to Matt last night, he confirmed Kevin's erratic behavior as a probable drug problem. Kevin has been harassing Matt and his mom for money and reacting violently if he is refused. Kevin has told me on the phone that he cries all the time and doesn't know why he's so miserable. He has dropped another course. He has come home most weekends without my knowledge. His coach suspects a drug problem. He actually admits to being an everyday stoner, but nothing past that. He lies, steals, and manipulates people for money. I have had little contact with CB, so he plays her for everything he can get. Matthew confirmed to me last night that the problem is drugs, not just homesickness. I need* to come up big now as a parent to help. Please help me to make the right moves now, for the right reasons, without anger and frustration. I think I need to do this despite how Kevin will react, which I expect will be badly.

> **Pray for Grace—followed by meditation.**
> **Answer:"Go to CB (Kevin's mom) and humbly ask for her assistance in solving this. An intervention seems to be the answer. It will take everyone out of denial; Kevin, CB, Matt, Laura, and I will all have to face the issue directly after the intervention. Kevin will not be able to continue his slide. School and lacrosse will take its proper place somehow. Don't worry about outside appearances when it comes to either school or lacrosse. We are at the crossroads."**

When I called CB, she confirmed that Kevin was addicted to pain killers. She talked to Kevin's girlfriend, Joy, and found out that Kevin has been doing Oxycontin on a regular basis. When I talked about an intervention, CB wanted it to be just the immediate family but vowed her cooperation. She knew better than I that Kevin was in big trouble and needed help. It felt good to be working together with her help on this.

On December 20, 2003, I asked the Holy Spirit for help, once again.

Question: *What is the next step in helping Kevin with the drug problem?*

My Thoughts: *Big day as far as Kevin's drug problem goes. I spoke to CB and she agreed that the problem exists. She talked to Joy (Kevin's girlfriend) who confirmed his drug abuse, using Oxycontin five times a week during the summer. She believed he had straightened out, but all indications are that he just lied effectively. I agreed with CB to have a small intervention with just her, Matt, and me but I believe that would be ineffective now. My intention is to bring in Joy, if she'd come, plus*

Laura, Bill Greeley, and Murf. I'm even considering Phyllie because of the effect it would have on him. I'm not sure of the post-intervention plan. Does he need to go to in-patient or out-patient rehab? Does he go back to school and play lacrosse? Do I move Kevin in with Laura and me? What has the best chance of success?

> **Pray for Grace—followed by meditation.**
> **Answer: "Be stronger than ever before. Your plan is sound. The right people will be there. See a drug counselor for post-intervention plans. Your spiritual practice has led you to handle this right. It's not about you, so don't get caught up in what others think. Be sensitive to CB but don't focus on her. She'll have to adjust. The awkwardness of being with Kevin over Christmas and not letting on about the intervention is just something that must be dealt with. This is what was meant to happen."**

****

It was a few days before Christmas when I contacted Kevin's girlfriend, Joy. I called and asked if we could meet and talk about Kevin. Joy was Kevin's first and only girlfriend at that time. She was a few years younger than Kevin and they had been together for about 4 years dating back to Kevin's senior year at Sherwood. Joy was now a student at Hofstra University but was home in Sherwood for the semester break. I asked her to keep the meeting secret and she agreed to meet me at a diner in Valley Stream.

Joy looked a bit nervous but she was willing and cooperative. She said she had threatened Kevin last summer that she was going to tell me all about his drug use, but Kevin begged her not to and promised to quit. She thought he had stopped at school, but realized when he returned that he hadn't. Although she had tears in her eyes, she was courageous in telling me details about the drug Oxycontin and how often Kevin used it. I asked her if she would be willing to attend an intervention to get Kevin to stop. Joy said she would do anything to help Kevin and was not afraid to go behind his back to help me in this effort.

I never had a daughter, but if I did I would want her to be like Joy. She had also experienced the effects of addiction in some loved ones, but she wanted no part of it. She seemed to love Kevin and was willing to make every effort to save him. I will never forget how greatly impressed I was by her strong character, integrity, and personal courage. Joy and I hugged each other as we left the diner and I expressed my gratitude for her help.

Laura helped me find some drug rehabs in the area by using the internet and I called and visited several to ask advice. They suggested that I set up an appointment for Kevin to go into rehab immediately following the intervention. Once I had a date for the rehab located an hour away, I made my plans for the intervention on December 29. By reading books on intervention and pamphlets from the rehab, I prepared to assemble a group that could convince Kevin to go to in-patient rehab out east on Long Island for a 28-day program. The plan included Kevin's returning to school on time to start the next semester and the beginning of the lacrosse season.

Matt was responsible for getting Kevin to my condo in Long Beach under the guise of eating dinner there. I assembled a contingent of ten people who Kevin liked and respected. There were three women including CB, Laura, and Joy. I asked my buddy Carl to come because he had experience with drug abuse in his step-son and was respected by Kevin. My assistant lacrosse coach, Bill Greeley, was there with whom Kevin was close. My buddy, Murf, who had lived with us in Sherwood was there. Coach Randazzo drove three hours from NU to help us convince Kevin to go into rehab.

I had put the Holy Spirit in charge and we were ready to get Kevin straight.

Chapter 18 –
Oxycontin

The first time I ever heard the word "Oxycontin" was from the news report that Rush Limbaugh, the conservative political radio personality, had become addicted to these powerful pain killers. Prescription pain killers just didn't sound like anything sinister and certainly not anything in the category of the most infamous of all drugs—heroin. Nevertheless, they are first cousins in the family of opiates and are equally addictive. I could imagine that people in pain could become addicted to the powerful relief that this opiate provides. It sounds like anyone who suffers terribly could innocently fall into the trap of a pain killer addiction. It is a most powerful pain killer designed for serious illnesses such as cancer.

I really knew nothing about the family of opiates or the illegal sale of prescription drugs for the sole purpose of getting sky high. The opiate users that Kevin met in college didn't pop the pills but broke them up into fine grain and snorted them like lines of cocaine. Unlike cocaine, however, you're not chasing that high all night by snorting more every half hour. Snort one 40mg. pill and you are flying for 5 hours or more with no diminishment. Opiates like Oxycontin are "downers" instead of stimulants like cocaine or speed. Kevin would later tell me he could sit on the couch not doing a thing and be happier than if he was scoring the winning goal of a championship game or scoring with the finest looking female on campus. He had found his new drug of choice, no question.

Later, there would be times when Kevin was in recovery that he would fully describe how much he loved the rush he would feel from snorting Oxycontin pills (henceforth referred to as OCs). One OC could cost $20-$30 and would keep Kevin high all night and leave him with enough left over in the morning to do a little more for an eye opener to start off his day. He started doing OCs during his junior year at NU but he hit full stride in this addiction on Long Island in the summer before his senior year. Somehow Kevin managed to work very little during the summer of 2003; but he still was able to get high on OC virtually every day and/or night.

Kevin didn't live with me that summer so I wasn't on top of how he spent his days and nights. I tried to line up a good summer job for him working for the Town of Hempstead Parks and Recreation. I had a few political connections and was encouraged that it wouldn't be any problem getting Kevin a job. But as days turned into weeks, Kevin still wasn't working. I finally found out that he never got the job because he never went in for the drug screening that was required for town government employment. When I confronted him, he said he was embarrassed to tell me because he knew he couldn't pass because he smoked pot. I was sick to my stomach at the thought of that, but marijuana was only the tip of the iceberg for Kevin. He was already addicted to prescription pain killers—the powerful opiate, Oxycontin.

He found a part time job delivering pizza with his own car, he told me. The truth was that the pizza delivery lasted a short time and Kevin was getting money from his mother every day for doing a few chores around the house. CB had landed a teaching job the year before and had some cash to lavish on her son. His mom wanted him to find a job, but Kevin managed to manipulate her for enough cash to support a $20-$30 a day drug habit—plus food, gas, cell phone, and other spending money. He could successfully avoid me by complaining that I always criticized him and looked for trouble. It was true. I was furious with him. He was out every night and slept past noon every day. He didn't even play lacrosse in the summer night leagues—the sport that he was so talented in and fully passionate about throughout his life.

When I did talk to him or see him, I'd chew him out for being such a bum. This led to a fight where neither of us showed any respect for the other. Because of the things that were being said and the tone of the arguments, we could not be around each other. That worked out very well for the continuance of Kevin's OC addiction. I knew that when I called him out on his laziness, he would react badly. If I was going to avoid a physical confrontation, I had to either accept him as he was or stay away. In my mind, my job as a father was to fix him. At the time, however, I didn't even understand the problem.

After one particularly bad discussion, he jumped out of my car and decided to walk a few miles home instead of listening to me anymore. I was totally frustrated that I couldn't even hold a conversation with him without a blow up. When I reached home, I asked the Holy Spirit for help. Within minutes I found myself once again on page 70 of ACIM, *Manual for Teachers*. It was a reminder that I must continue to turn this over to my Higher Power. And once again, it gave the best advice I could ever have.

> **"Ask and He will answer. The responsibility is His, and He alone is fit to assume it. To do so is His function. To refer questions to Him is yours. Would you want to be responsible for decisions about which you understand so little? Be glad you have a Teacher Who cannot make a mistake. His answers are always right. Can you say that of yours?**

I was reminded that I had help whenever I needed it. Holy Spirit's advice is infallible but it takes belief in that in order to accept His guidance. The more difficult Kevin's situation became, the more I found myself turning to my Inner Guidance. Following this guidance requires trust. The more I practiced turning to Holy Spirit, the stronger my trust was to become.

****

Although during this summer I had no knowledge of Oxycontin, I knew something was wrong. It became known that summer that Kevin was not going to graduate on time from NU and also that he was not going to graduate with a teaching certification at all. Kevin had wanted to be a teacher and coach his whole life, but he didn't care about it anymore. He seemed to have lost his soul completely, but I still didn't have a grip on what the cause was yet.

Kevin went back to NU at the end of the summer for his senior year. CB was glad to get rid of him because he had become a nightmare to live with. She had spent a small fortune to support him and it was a constant struggle to get him to do anything constructive. His brother, Matt, was giving him a wide berth as well in order to avoid a fight. At the time, Kevin had successfully deceived Matt and CB about his addiction, and although they had suspicions, they had no concrete evidence. Kevin's relationship with both of them was also at an all time low by the time of the intervention.

Chapter 19 –
Intervention

Everyone had successfully kept the secret of Kevin's upcoming intervention. Although it seemed deceptive, we all knew it was necessary. Kevin had to be caught completely off guard and confronted with his problem in front of the people he loves and respects most. Matt didn't really relish his job of bringing Kevin into an "ambush" but accepted the fact that we were all there to help Kevin, not hurt him.

The procedure we agreed on was to ask Kevin to listen to each one of us without any comment. Each person there was to explain to Kevin that he/she loved him and was there because he needed help. I would serve as the group's leader and would set the tone by telling Kevin that we know about his addiction to the drug Oxycontin and that we were all here because of the danger of his addiction. I would tell the story of how I perceived his addiction affecting his life, my life, and our family as a whole. I was to be followed by his mom CB, his brother Matt, his girlfriend Joy, and my wife Laura. They would tell Kevin how much he was loved but also how his addiction was adversely affecting them. They would finish by asking Kevin to go to the 28-day program at the Suffolk County Center for Recovery (SCCR).

Bill Greeley was Kevin's coach and my assistant throughout his high school years. He had a great relationship with Kevin and I knew Kevin would respect his opinion. My friend Carl had a step son who was a heroin addict. He would tell his story of how his kid has lived as an addict and devastated everyone in his family. Murf would go next. Murf had lived with us in Sherwood and was considered by Kevin to be "the world's best guy." Murf also had addiction run rampant in his family and would tell Kevin through his experience of how bad the end of this road was on which he was traveling. Coach Greg Randazzo was there to tell Kevin that he could turn everything around by going into a 28-day rehab program that was waiting for him and would have a recovery program in place at NU when he returned to the school and to his team. The timing was perfect for Kevin to return for the first day of the spring semester and to practice for his final season of college lacrosse.

My belief was that Kevin would melt in front of all this love and opportunity that was presented to him. I didn't see how he could resist the logical and loving presentation of his problem and the obvious solution. But I completely miscalculated Kevin's reaction by underestimating the drug's power.

From the time Kevin walked into my living room and saw the assembly of the people there, his eyes blazed a fire of seeming hatred towards me for putting him in this situation. He did love and respect all the people in the room, but he decided that this was his controlling father's devious scheme and was braced to reject it.

Everyone in the room played his/her part perfectly and I thought that Kevin's anger and resentment was easing a little with every speaker. I believed when Coach Randazzo had finished with explaining the opportunity to return to school and the team for a glorious final season as a senior, Kevin would be relieved and gratefully accept.

When I asked Kevin to speak and give us an answer to the proposition, he simply shook his head and said there was no way he needed a rehab. He denied any extensive drug use and refused to go. I think everyone there was in shock.

The rest of the night was spent by each individual meeting with Kevin in a separate room to talk to him and hear his side of the story. Kevin's denials were convincing to many of the people there. Some actually wondered if we had exaggerated the problem and overreacted with the intervention. But I knew he was lying. I felt sick to my stomach that he hadn't acquiesced to the proposal of going immediately into recovery. The timing was perfect. He had to go now or I couldn't send him back to school. Kevin stayed downstairs with his girlfriend while everyone slowly left. They all wished me luck and reiterated how much they love Kevin and would do anything to help him.

Once the people were gone, Joy had a chance to work on him alone. I don't know how she did it but by morning, Kevin admitted he had a problem and was ready to go immediately to SCCR for the 28-day program. CB packed a bag for him and Matt brought it over. I realized quickly that Joy was the key to this and asked her to please come with Kevin and me for the ride out to Southampton. She eagerly agreed.

On the hour long ride, Kevin was in a confession mode. He described the full extent of his drug use. He spoke of how it first began at NU snorting OCs but that he found he could get the pills cheaper down on Long Island. That explained his frequent weekend trips home. He admitted that he used OCs on occasion as a junior in college but it was last summer while at home that he used it every day. The high he got would last for several hours without any let up in intensity. The pills would be broken up into a fine powder and snorted through a straw. He would leave a small amount for the morning when he awoke to start off his day. The more he did the OCs, the more he needed to get high. He figured he had a $30-40 a day habit and was always trying to get money to keep his habit going. Kevin had finally admitted to coming into my place in Long Beach and stealing money from my change jar. Most of the money, however, he either stole or received from his mom. Kevin seemed relieved to be confessing all this to me and I think we both believed during the ride that everything was going to be okay now.

When we pulled up to Suffolk County Center for Recovery (SCCR), however, things started to get a bit tense. We sat in the small lobby for a while waiting to be seen and it seemed with each passing minute Kevin's good attitude towards recovery diminished quickly. We met with a nurse who asked Kevin a series of questions about his drug use and Kevin seemed to be hedging on his answers.

We were asked to wait inside the kitchen where they had coffee and I tried to tell Kevin how good this was going to be for him.

At just that moment, we could hear a furious woman screaming curses and threatening violence at one of the people working at the rehab. She was probably going through a tough withdrawal—at least that's what I was thinking, and the sound of her shrill voice sent a chill down my spine. I looked at Kevin and I saw the anger and fear starting to build. He said, "Let's get the fuck out of here; I'm not staying here." Just then a rehab administrator came and said that they had a room ready and we were to say goodbye to Kevin. Joy kissed Kevin through her tears and I gave him a big hug and told him everything would be alright. Joy and I could both sense that Kevin wasn't ready for this but we hoped for the best.

On the way home, Joy and I talked about how Kevin's drug use had a negative effect on their relationship and on his entire attitude. Kevin, she said, didn't care about anything anymore except getting high. She said Kevin didn't blame her for cooperating with us in our efforts to get Kevin clean but Kevin was going to blame everyone except himself for being railroaded into going to rehab starting that night.

Chapter 20 –
Inpatient Rehab

I did not do a thorough study of drug rehabs before I chose the Suffolk County Center for Recovery out east on Long Island. I picked one that accepted my insurance and was within reasonable driving distance. The way I understood the recovery process was that it did not matter whether or not it was high priced or a low budget rehab; it all depended on the readiness of the drug addict to surrender his disease to a Higher Power and commit to the Twelve Step program. I later found out that this wasn't a universally shared philosophy. Even so, no rehab can guarantee success at any price.

In the first 3 nights of Kevin's program of rehabilitation, he called me no less than 20 times demanding that I come pick him up. During the first 3 nights, Kevin was going through detox, so I figured that was the reason for his obnoxious and incessant harassment of me, his mother, brother, and friends. Kevin did not consider himself to be a drug addict and seemed to truly believe he was the victim of an overbearing father who overreacted to a normal son who just liked to party.

Sunday was visitors' day at SCCR and when I arrived Joy was already there. She took me aside before I saw Kevin and described to me Kevin's attitude. Kevin had told the people in the "group" session that he may never do Oxycontin again, but he sure as hell was not going to quit drinking and smoking pot for the rest of his life at 20 years old. The counselor calmly told Kevin in front of the group that he might have to come back many times before he understood that he must abstain from all intoxicants. The counselor would prove to be a prophet.

When I met with Kevin, he was civil to me despite the terrible verbal assaults I had received from him over the phone that week. He calmly and politely proclaimed himself cured, promised he would never do OCs again, and insisted he was not going to learn anything he didn't already know from "these people." He denounced "them" as real drug addicts and Kevin considered himself to be more like a misunderstood party boy saddled with a domineering father.

There was nothing stopping Kevin from leaving the rehab on his own except for the absence of a ride back to his mom's house in Merrick. When Joy and I both refused to take him, he turned nasty and harassed me all the way to the door. It had not yet been a week, so I was praying that something or someone in rehab would help him to see the light. So far the only thing stopping him from bolting the place was his lack of a ride home. I had told him that if he did leave, he was not going back to Northern University. That might have been the real reason he was still there.

Ten days later I returned to SCCR to meet with Kevin's counselor, Mike Jones. Mike was a 300 lb. African-American with a big smile and warm personality. I met with Mike before Kevin came in to join us. Mike said that Kevin was in total denial, angry, frustrated, and focused only on getting out. He convinced me that accepting recovery would be completely Kevin's choice—not mine or anyone else's. If Kevin continued with this attitude, he wouldn't learn anything. But he said that every day that he stays is a chance to make a breakthrough and that chance is almost non-existent outside of the rehab.

When Kevin came into join us, he showed a slightly disrespectful attitude towards me. Mike immediately admonished him for this disrespect and let him know that he would have felt so incredibly blessed if he had a father who cared this much about him when he was a young man in the grip of addiction. He gave the credit for his recovery to the grace of God, the Twelve Steps, and the love of his counselors. Believing his life was saved by this combination, he devoted himself to helping others.

I could tell that Kevin had respect for this big man and he apologized to Mike for the disrespect he showed towards his father in his presence. It was apparent that the two men liked one another, and although Kevin was resistant to treatment, he listened to his counselor with admiration. Mike used the metaphor, "You can bring a horse to water, but you can't make him drink." He predicted that someday Kevin would understand what he cannot accept now and would be appreciative of the fact that I was there to try and help.

Kevin was still angry at me when I left . . . but something had just happened there. I couldn't put my finger on it, but I sensed a shift. When I returned to SCCR four days later, he was different. He still wanted out of the place but he had lost the anger and the sense that he had been unjustly treated. I asked him a few questions concerning the Twelve Steps but he didn't show any real understanding of their value. There was still a week left of the 28-day program and I was hoping for a breakthrough.

When I returned home, I meditated on my meeting with Kevin and asked my Higher Power for guidance. I received this response and wrote it in my journal.

> *"You're not doing all this spiritual work for nothing. Kevin is a true test for you to turn everything over to God. It is also a test for you to treat everyone involved with kindness, compassion, and without judgment . . . forgiving those whom you think have wronged you. Let go of any feelings of personal victimization of having a drug addicted son who is not grateful for all that has been given to him or done for him. It's a chance to put all the things you've learned into practice—not only with Kevin, but with others. Let go of the need to have it turn out a certain way. The BIG PICTURE cannot be seen from this view right now. Let go and let God. Everything you have learned should be practiced now."*

The next night when I was supervising a varsity basketball game at Sherwood HS, I got a call from Kevin saying he was on his way home. He had convinced his mother that 18 days was enough time in rehab, so she picked him up in front of the SCCR building without going inside. I called SCCR and they confirmed that he had left the program "against medical advice." Despite all the spiritual help I had received from Holy Spirit, I let the rage take me over. I called CB's cell phone and fumed over the seeming betrayal. She had concluded that Kevin had enough treatment and was ready to return to school. I threw every guilt trip I could think of at her. It became obvious that I was not following my Inner Teacher's advice to "let go and let God."

I had told Kevin that if he left treatment early, I would take away his car and not pay his tuition for school. In truth, his tuition was already paid but I still held the power of the purse over money for food and the car. I felt terribly depressed and knew I needed to turn my feelings and the situation over to Holy Spirit, my Higher Power.

****

Question: *What do I do now that Kevin has left rehab before he completed the 28 day program?*

My Thoughts: *Kevin left rehab—talked CB into picking him up. I expressed strong disagreement with CB about picking him up without his being released by the counselors at SCCR. I feel anger and disappointment still with Kevin, and now with CB. I don't know how to handle the situation from here, especially concerning the car. My relationship with Kevin is not improved, nor is my relationship with CB—now that he left early with her help. I need direction now. I've learned to make the right moves now by giving a big effort to turn everything over to God. Please help me to be the best father possible in this difficult situation.*

> **Pray for Grace—followed by meditation.**
> **Answer: "You still feel anger and disappointment and believe that what you want to say and do will only be seen as punitive and controlling. You don't want to control Kevin anymore and you want to make that clear to him.**

> *Although he won't believe that, it is true. It is impossible for you not to want to control how his car is used and abused when you are responsible for everything bad that might happen. Therefore, give ownership of the car to Kevin. He will get his own insurance but you will pay it until June. You will also pay his room, board, books, and tuition through December. After that, he's on his own. If he wants your advice, friendship and love—you want to be there for him, but only if he asks. You want no control over his partying habits, his academic or athletic performance. You'll pay through December—but his performance is his own. Don't give Kevin cash anymore. This should feel fair to you. Remember, whatever he thinks about you now doesn't matter. What he thinks 15 years from now will."*

Again, my Inner Guidance, my Higher Self, has clearly directed me to let go of trying to control him. Sometimes I listen, sometimes I don't.

Chapter 21 –
Senior Year at NU

When Kevin returned to Northern University after leaving recovery ten days before finishing the program, I did not have confidence that he had changed his attitude but hoped for the best. This was his senior year as a NU lacrosse player, and for our family it was to be the culmination of many years of closely following Kevin in sports competition. Was Kevin going to ruin this by relapsing with drugs?

Coach Randazzo was there to keep a close eye on him, so we would know pretty soon whether or not Kevin was on the straight and narrow. The word from his coaches was that Kevin was totally focused and playing well. He announced to all his teammates at a team meeting that he had just been in rehab for an opiate addiction to Oxycontin and that he could not drink, smoke pot, or do any intoxicants. He explained that he needed to be totally committed to his team and would not let them down. His teammates now had the responsibility of helping him keep that commitment.

Laura was busy with a family obligation for the first game of the season, so my friend and assistant coach, Bill Greeley, accompanied me down South to watch Kevin play as a starter at the attack position against the University of North Carolina. The Tar Heels were an excellent team and NU was unfortunately not on top of its game that day, suffering a 12-7 loss. Kevin played okay but not great. I was concerned with how he would handle the loss, considering that he had never been a good loser.

Coach Greeley and I got to talk with Kevin for a while after the game and he seemed fine. He was thrilled to see that Bill made the long trip with me to support him, and he appreciated the fact that he was even playing, considering the ordeal he had recently been through. We both told him how proud we were of him and all the good things his coaches had said. I had arranged our Sherwood HS lacrosse schedule so that I would be able to travel to his games. Kevin appeared proud of himself and upbeat despite the disappointing loss. Bill and I returned to NY thrilled to see Kevin in such good shape.

The following week Kevin was on fire in a Tuesday game against Hartford in Connecticut. He broke a 5-5 tie at halftime by scoring four consecutive 3rd quarter goals and the team went on to win 13-7. Kevin finished the game with a career high, six goals and two assists. The following Saturday he scored two more goals in a win against Stony Brook and was chosen as the "Athlete of the Week" for all sports at Northern University.

We were all so thrilled and, of course, so was Coach Randazzo, who got a little choked up when he was presenting Kevin with the plaque at an awards luncheon of athletes, coaches, and administrators. It seemed like everyone could feel that a success story was taking place here. At that moment, I believed that Kevin was in better shape mentally, emotionally, and physically than at any time in his life. I was filled with gratitude.

The following week NU lost a close game to Harvard. Kevin came out to dinner with Laura and me and he seemed great, despite the loss. We shared some important conversation about drugs, addiction, the Twelve Steps, and the possibility of his moving into our small beach condo with us. He also said he wanted to take 6 credits up at NU over the summer to make sure he graduated by the end of the fall semester in December. Kevin, however, had not been attending any AA or NA meetings as he had promised, but he convinced us that between school and lacrosse, there was little time. He said that NU lacrosse was his recovery program. With all the success we were witnessing, Laura and I were just grateful to have Kevin so happy and healthy. We didn't want to push. Although

I could not help but wonder how it was all going to turn out, I reminded myself that Holy Spirit had clearly told me that I was not in charge of his recovery. That is a lot easier to remember when things are going well, however. I thanked and praised God for these wonderful weeks since Kevin had left rehab. On the way home from NU, Laura and I enjoyed talking about how he seemed like a totally different young man. The next week Kevin scored four goals at Penn State in a big 17-8 win for NU. Things were so good now. Kevin looked so happy and, of course, so were we.

****

How fast things change. Laura was away in Tokyo on a business trip and I went up to NU by myself on a Friday night to see the game against Manhattan College under the lights. CB and Matt also went up in a separate car and I met them there. Kevin had planned to ride home to Long Island with me because the school was out of session for the holiday weekend. I was excited about taking that ride home together.

The Manhattan team had a couple of players with whom Kevin had formerly been teammates in both Sherwood and in Merrick. One of the fathers had actually coached Kevin in Little League when the kids were about 9 or 10. When I saw the fathers of these boys in the stands, they were complimentary about how well Kevin was playing this season. We promised each other that we would get together with the boys after the game.

NU blew out Manhattan 16-4 however Kevin didn't play well and was shut out with no goals or assists. After the game I became embarrassed that Kevin never showed up to see the kids and parents who were waiting to share congratulations and tell some old stories about when they were all little kids together. I could tell when Kevin left the field that he was upset, but I didn't expect him to leave the stadium without saying hello to his mom, brother, and the other families who were looking forward to a little reunion to chat about old times.

I apologized to all about Kevin's unexplained disappearance. Since Kevin had planned to ride home to Long Island with me, I called him to see what happened. He said to come to his house to pick him up but wouldn't answer why he had left abruptly without saying hello to everyone. His tone was angry. I told CB and Matt that Kevin was in a foul mood, it seemed, and that I would drive him to CB's house in Merrick and see if I could figure out what's up with him.

When I reached Kevin's apartment he was ready with his bag and immediately jumped in the car. I asked him why he bolted out of the stadium when there were so many people who wanted to see him. He went into a rant about how Coach Randazzo pulled him out of the game and how unfairly he was treated. Although I didn't agree with his evaluation of the situation, I focused on the fact that he was being selfish in not caring about the people who wanted to see him after the game. And after all, his team had won big and he was now acting like a little brat because he wasn't the star of the game this time.

He then turned all his anger on me. In the nastiest language he could muster, he said he knew I wouldn't care about how he felt. I would stick up for Coach Randazzo and blame him for not behaving like a perfect player. He said that I only cared about myself and how I looked in front of these people. He screamed, "Don't give me this bullshit about how much you care about me. You only give a shit about how you look. I don't care what the fuck they say or whether or not they're happy with me. Fuck Randazzo, fuck them, and fuck you too! Call mom and tell her I want to go home in her car. And you know something; you're a real piece of shit."

I wasn't ready for that at all. I pulled the car over on the side of Route 9 and screamed at him to get out. He responded, "I'm not getting out until I know mom is coming." He then sat there defiantly as he started to call his mom on his cell phone. I grabbed a hold of him and tried to push him out of the passenger door, screaming at him to get out. When I couldn't move him out the door from that angle, I flew out of the driver's side door around to the passenger door, opened it, and tried to pull him out of the car. He resisted but I was determined that there was no way he was staying in my car. We smacked each other pretty good in the tussle but eventually I got his hands released from whatever he was holding on to, and we rolled to the ground on the side of the road. Kevin was furious but he moved away from me quickly and around to the other side of the car. I quickly dove in through the passenger side to grab the keys from the ignition before he could get them.

Standing there on the side of the road, totally exhausted and angrier now at myself than at him, I called CB and told her that she had to turn back and come get Kevin before I kill him. When she asked what happened, I responded, "Just get here quick before something worse happens." I explained where we were and it took about 10 minutes before CB and Matt pulled up next to us. For those 10 minutes Kevin leered at me as if he never hated anyone more in his life. We didn't say another word but his look was demonic.

When CB and Matt arrived they could see from the look of us that something was very wrong. Kevin immediately jumped into his mom's car and I told Matt to ride home with me. I was physically and emotionally drained and I barely said a word to Matt for the three hour drive home. I was ashamed of myself for losing control and responding with violence. All the way home I was thinking about all the concepts that I'd learned from *A Course in Miracles* and how I threw them away the second I felt attacked. I wondered, "What good is studying all this stuff if it's not going to work for me when I need it?"

I drove home slowly either because I was exhausted or depressed. I thought about how Kevin would get home before us—take his mother's car, go find his friends and get high. When Matt and I pulled up to his mom's house in Merrick, CB's car wasn't there. Matt went inside and found that his mom was in bed and Kevin had taken the car as I predicted. It was 1AM.

I was alone when I got back to Long Beach because Laura was in Tokyo. What a miserable night that was!

****

The Glenz family has been known to get into some physical, violent, and emotional confrontations over the years—but we also forgive and forget pretty quickly. Kevin and I both felt badly about the way we reacted and we were both interested in putting it behind us as quickly as we could. We apologized to each other and wanted to go back to how we were before the blow-up. Fortunately Kevin was still in lacrosse season, so the following week Laura and I went down to Georgetown University to watch a game that would determine if NU would make it into the NCAA playoff picture.

Kevin played, perhaps his best college game, scoring four goals and keeping the game close. When it ended, the Hoyas of Georgetown had held off a late NU rally to win a tight contest. We were sad for the Northern team that their playoff hopes were gone with one game left in the season but we were happy that Kevin played so well against such impressive competition again.

A week later, we went up to NU for the last game against Rutgers. It was a strong win for Northern and a sad day for us as this marked the end of Kevin's college lacrosse career. We all went to the team party following the season and Kevin and I wound up in an uncomfortable argument when he told me he wasn't staying up at NU over the summer semester to catch up on 6 credits so he could graduate by December.

There was also a keg of beer at the party—Kevin was now 21 and legal—and I knew he wanted me to leave so he could party hardy. He never did believe that he would ever remain a straight arrow. Now, with the season over, he was ready to lay back and cut loose. He didn't want to hear any questions about whether he had drank or smoked pot during the season or if he intended to now. Laura had to split us up because she could see how this was going.

On the drive home I had a premonition that big trouble was on the way.

Chapter 22 –
Pains of Relapse

———◆———

While Kevin was away visiting his cousins in California, I took CB to dinner one night to talk about both Matt and Kevin. Because I had a strong tendency to tell her how to treat Kevin, especially when it came to his drug use, CB was not usually too interested in what I had to say to her. I was trying to be less judgmental with her, knowing how she loves Kevin and how tough it is to live with him. She was doing the best she could in a difficult situation. Somehow I didn't have her trust to confide in me about everything that was going on with him.

My mom was now deteriorating with the dementia / Alzheimer's. She required a lot of attention from me and that was a big change in our relationship. I had spent my whole life admiring my mother's emotional strength and her compassion for others. I don't really think I have ever respected anyone more than Phyllie. It was difficult to recognize her as the same woman. I know it's a disease that progresses and none of it was her fault, yet it was tough to watch that happen. Between Kevin and my mom, I had a lot of bad thoughts flowing in and out of me all day and night.

Worst of all, Laura told me through heavy tears that she couldn't take it anymore. She had been wonderful about Phyllie and was always there for her. She had also given all she could to help and support Kevin, but had received little thanks back for all her efforts. It was my apparent depression over both Phyllie and Kevin that made her completely miserable. She wanted to see a psychologist so she could deal with her feelings. She said she couldn't continue to live with all this every day. I never expected this. Of everyone in my life, she was the most dependable and understanding. Now even she was falling apart.

I spent a lot of time in prayer and meditation those days looking for answers. I know that ACIM teaches me that I create everything that happens to me with the power of my own thoughts. It says that everything that I experience in this life is "an outside picture of an inner condition." This is a tough metaphysical concept for me to understand, but deep inside I seem to know that this is the truth. How could I use this kind of knowledge to help me? The answer, according to ACIM, is to turn all my problems and concerns over to the Holy Spirit, my Higher Power, the Universal Self.

"Wasn't I doing that?" I asked Holy Spirit. The answer I got said, "**You ask and then go and do whatever you think might fix it without listening to the answer from your Higher Self.**" And I know that is true. How many times have I been told that it is not my job to fix everyone? I can accept everyone as they are and love them anyway. Easier said than done—and I was not doing a good job at getting that done. If, as ACIM says, everything I see in the world comes from my own thoughts—my thoughts must be pretty screwed up.

****

On Father's Day we found out that Kevin was back to snorting OCs. We got most of the information from his girlfriend, Joy. Apparently he was just as addicted as before. Kevin had gone crazy a few times when he hadn't been able to get the drug. It's a strong addiction and he couldn't stay away from it. I asked again for Divine Guidance.

Contemplation on 6/21/04

Question: *Kevin is back on OC. What should be my plan in the resolution?*

My Thoughts: Kevin is obviously back on OC. He looks terrible and his actions are just like before. He probably began right after the season, but possibly before. He's constantly lying to me, denying any drug use. I need to be firm but not lose my compassion in the face of the verbal / physical onslaught that will occur when I take away everything—car, insurance, tuition and rent at NU. Please give me guidance.

> ***Pray for grace—followed by meditation***
> ***Answer: "Use your ability to talk to his friends—Jack, Jim, even Bobby. Ask them to help you save Kevin from his serious drug addiction. Don't be threatening but be straightforward, honest, and see what results come out of it. It's a bold, proactive move but will yield results."***

I called two of Kevin's best friends whom I had taught and coached in high school. Both agreed to meet me. I met each of them separately in the Sherwood HS parking lot and took each one for a ride. Jimmy seemed nervous; he didn't want to be an informer to his friend's father but he did want to help. When I told him that Kevin was back on OC, he acted surprised. He mentioned that Kevin often left the group for periods of time and returned later. Jimmy said that if Kevin was doing OC, he wasn't doing it with any of his old friends.

Jack was also willing to go for a ride with me. Jack was not at all intimidated by me asking questions about Kevin's drug use. Jack had tried snorting OC a few times but it tended to make him sick to his stomach. He admitted that he believed Kevin was back on it but said that Kevin stayed away from him when he did it. Jack confessed that he was a big drinker, pot smoker, and occasionally he'd do some cocaine—but he said that OC is bad news and he didn't doubt that Kevin was in trouble. He stressed how much he loved Kevin and vowed to help me anytime and in any way he could.

I did a lot of meditation over the next week and received messages reminding me to let God do all the work—directing me to be His instrument. These affirmations allowed me to handle Kevin's drug problem with considerable strength. Laura, however, continued to break down under this pressure and was receiving help from a psychologist. I wished all this heartache didn't have to be such a big part of her life. Laura couldn't have known what she signed up for when she decided to marry me. It seemed that as soon as we were married, my mom fell apart with Alzheimer's and my son became an opiate addict. Although I normally would have felt guilty, I knew that this was karma for her that she had to experience, the same way it was for me. We were going to have to grow from this together. And that was certainly what would happen.

I found a highly recommended local drug rehab center called Pemto, and I called and explained the situation. Dr. Barry Lipsky had an outstanding reputation in the field of drug addiction and I was pleased when he contacted me after my first call. Dr. Lipsky, or Barry as we were to refer to him, strongly suggested that CB and I both be there with Kevin for their first meeting. CB has never been comfortable in this kind of situation and I knew she would be resistant. Barry insisted that CB be there, however, since it was her house where Kevin was living. After some hesitation, CB agreed to contact the Pemto Center and try to arrange for a meeting.

Getting Kevin to go to the meeting would be much more challenging. Making it more difficult was the fact that in two days, Laura and I were going to Japan as group leaders of another educational tour with 6 students from Sherwood High School. If we didn't get this done immediately, we would delay Kevin's recovery plan by more than two weeks. I still had one ace up my sleeve to force Kevin to attend. Although I tried to give Kevin the car to put into his own name—it never got done. So the car still was in my name and I could take it away. If Kevin refused to attend the meeting with Dr. Lipsky, I threatened to take the car. After much abusive protest, Kevin caved in and said he would attend.

Just hours before the meeting I did a contemplation asking for Holy Spirit's help.

Question: *What is the best action that I can take concerning Kevin's relapse into Oxycontin addiction?*

My thoughts: Right now, my relationship with Kevin is at an all-time low. He hates me and thinks that I hate him. I've exposed his drug problem to his family and peers; I've taken away his car and his college tuition. I urged his mom to do the same. CB, Kevin, and I are meeting in two hours at Pemto for an evaluation of Kevin's problem. I'm going to Japan tomorrow. I followed the advice of the last contemplation and am again asking for Divine Guidance.

> *Pray for Grace—followed by meditation*
> *Answer: "Make no plans for the future with Kevin. There will be more upset and heartache in the near future concerning his drug problem. You just be as kind, loving, and non-judgmental as possible. Focus on showing Kevin that you love him, despite his drug addiction. That is your only direction and only plan right now. It is not an easy one for you. It will test your level of consciousness as nothing yet has—but you are ready."*

The evaluation meeting with Barry started off well. He asked Kevin a lot of detailed questions about drugs and drug use that I never heard of before. Kevin admitted to a lot of experience with these drugs in the past and he opened up honestly confessing to things which I never knew. Kevin admitted only to drinking and smoking pot at first, but then admitted to snorting a few OCs on a couple of occasions.

Everything looked good until Barry made his recommendation that Kevin immediately take a drug screening then and there. Kevin refused. Barry then recommended that Kevin go to another 28-day program in an expensive in-patient facility. Kevin glared at the doctor and just shook his head. Barry relented a bit and said Kevin could choose to swear total abstinence of all drinking and all drugs with the out-patient program testing him.

Kevin said, "No way. This is a set up. I never agreed to any of this." CB told Barry that she didn't see any problem with a 22 year old man drinking a few beers and smoking a little pot. Barry looked at CB and said, "You are doing your son a tremendous disservice with that statement." CB immediately left the room and the Pemto facility without another word. Kevin followed her out.

Alone with the doctor, I asked him what he would suggest. He said that Kevin was taking a very dangerous drug and he needed to go to a better rehab than the previous one. I told him that I would be away for two weeks and asked what I should do now. He suggested that I take away his car and not to send him back to school to finish the last 18 credits he needed to graduate. He emphasized that Kevin first must have at least 6 months of clean drug screens. He firmly stated that Kevin's life was in danger and he was putting others in equal danger by driving a car.

I left the Pemto facility more confused than ever before. The doctor was telling me I had to act immediately with all the leverage I had on him. It was my responsibility, he said, to do everything possible in my power to stop this downward spiral. He again stressed that my son had a disease and that the only cure was total abstinence. If he drank or smoked pot, he would most certainly find his way back to Oxycontin—his true drug of choice.

The phone calls started from Kevin before I even left Barry Lipsky's office. He again screamed that he was set up. He said he was always going to be drinking and doing drugs. The other way was just too boring. And, of course, he wanted his car back. After all, he attended the meeting. I told him it was irresponsible to give the car to a drug addict and reiterated what Barry had said. The choice was to go into a 28-day in-patient program or to swear total abstinence of all drugs. The second choice required going to the out-patient clinic at Pemto and taking drug screens several times a week. Kevin completely flipped out.

He called me several times an hour to harass me and repeated he would always drink and smoke pot. He knew that deep down I believed if he was only doing that, it wouldn't be so bad. But I knew Kevin was snorting OCs and had no intention of stopping. I hid the car in Long Beach and put a security club on the steering wheel so it couldn't be moved. The phone calls continued on my cell and house phone. This had a bad effect on Laura and we were fortunate to be leaving the country the next day for two weeks in Japan.

I met CB in Long Beach to see if I could get her help. She admitted she could not handle the kid and that he was never going to go back to rehab. She now had the pressure of him wanting her car all the time. CB was angry that I was leaving her with all the headaches while I went away to Japan. On the 14 hour flight to Osaka I thought about little else.

****

I spent a lot of my trip to Japan thinking about Kevin. I said a prayer in front of every statue of Buddha and at every Shinto shrine I saw. Every prayer seemed to be answered by a similar message: **"Kevin has got to go through his own karma. I can't change this and shouldn't try to interfere."** It was a frustrating message for me. Barry Lipsky clearly told me that I had to act decisively and immediately. This drug is too dangerous. Kevin was a risk to himself and others. To do less was to be irresponsible. And Dr. Lipsky had an outstanding reputation for being one of the best in his field.

The night I returned home from Japan, Kevin called me at 1AM. With the time difference and jet lag, I was wide awake. He said he wanted to talk seriously tomorrow but his words sounded slurred to me. Being conflicted between my advice from professionals in the field of drug abuse and Holy Spirit, I turned again to my Higher Power for further clarification.

****

Question / focus: *I'm asking for firm guidelines in advising Kevin tomorrow. Certainly the car and paying for school are the two issues I control. How do I play my cards in the most loving and compassionate way to help my son with his dangerous disease?*

My thoughts: *Kevin has a disease; he's in denial and can't see a clear picture out of the world of drugs and drinking. How could he? Those around him, who love him, also can't imagine a world without drinking parties. He's known nothing else. Neither have I. Do I stop all drinking as well—knowing it would further my spiritual path and strengthen*

Kevin's will to succeed also? I need help to stay calm, focused, loving, and compassionate. I'm willing to do anything to help him—but, Lord, I need to stay focused on Your direction. I turn this Holy Instant over to You. You lead and I will follow, knowing that Your direction will bring me peace.

> **Pray for Grace—followed by meditation**
> **Answer: "Encourage Kevin to go into a 28-day program and to move in with you and Laura after he comes out. Explain this to him by using methods you have learned from your spiritual path by showing compassion for Kevin's fear of this radical lifestyle change for him. Offer to make this change of complete abstinence yourself, specifically in your house while Kevin lives there. Make a ledger of pros and cons for quitting all drugs and encourage Kevin to also make the same ledger. Compare the two ledgers. Stay firm on the car and college payments. Encourage Kevin to accept responsibility for making more money, maintaining his car, treating your condo with respect, and developing more self discipline in his personal habits. Stay firm and don't be manipulated by Kevin's button pushing when he comes hard at you. If Kevin is not ready now, he will be someday; so be patient and understand this when he resists now. But stay firm and keep turning this over to God. His direction will bring you peace."**

****

Getting Kevin to go to another 28-day program seemed unlikely, unless I had CB's support. But CB's support didn't seem forthcoming until Kevin completely frightened her with one of his insane rages. CB had gone into the hospital for some surgery and upon her return home, Kevin was furious at Matt for ratting him out on letting people in her house while she was away. As a full fist fight broke out between the two brothers in the kitchen, CB tried to break it up and subsequently got shoved to the floor violently by

Kevin. She feared she had torn open her stitches from the surgery and started screaming. Defending his sister, CB's brother Stephen stepped into the melee against Kevin. At some point Kevin must have panicked and pulled a steak knife from the draw, brandishing it against the other three in the kitchen. CB called 911 and Kevin quickly fled from the house.

CB called me before the police arrived and pleaded for me to do something about Kevin and that she feared for her safety. It appeared that her brother, Stephen, had gotten the worst of the beatings, but all three seemed pretty shaken up by the whole scene of Kevin's wild-eyed rampage. When I arrived at the house, the police were taking their report but CB said she did not want to press charges; she just wanted Kevin to stay out of the house. The police informed CB that they could arrest him if he came into her house again.

This was actually the break I needed. Without CB, Kevin was homeless, without a car, and without any money. As long as CB was scared of him, she wouldn't renege on her decision to keep him out of the house. Knowing how successful Kevin was in manipulating his mom in the past, I realized I had to move fast before she changed her mind. Kevin was on foot but with a cell phone. I called him and explained the situation about the police and his mother's promise to have him arrested if he returned to her house in Merrick. Kevin seemed out of his mind—ranting about Matt's betrayal of him, his hatred of Stephen, and his mom's overreaction of the scene. I offered to pick him up if he wanted to talk about it. Not knowing where else to turn, he took my offer and I told him I would pick him up in 15 minutes.

Before I left, I told CB that this was probably a reaction from being dope sick (i.e. not being able to score the drug). She was still shook up and eagerly jumped at the idea of putting him in another rehab—actually anything to get him away from her. This all sounded good to me, but I knew CB's propensity for forgiving Kevin once things had settled down. I asked Matt to make sure he doesn't get back in the house. Matt just seemed sad at the whole state of affairs. He was upset that his brother thought he had betrayed him, but more so because Kevin acted like a dope crazed lunatic.

When I met up with Kevin, he was filled with hatred. We drove around for a long time with him heaping verbal abuse at me with no seeming end in sight. I knew that I couldn't lose my cool now; this was the moment to get him to go to rehab. I couldn't take him home to my house because he would scare Laura. We continued to drive for hours, stopping only at a McDonald's to get burgers and fries. I presented his only alternatives as: 1–homelessness and poverty; 2–jail; and 3–detox, rehab, and recovery.

This was to be about eight hours of hell for both of us. At one point he got out of the car and left me. After a few minutes of giving up on him, I realized I had to make the most out of this situation while it existed. I drove around the neighborhood where he had gotten out until I found him on his cell phone screaming at someone. When he hung up, I asked him if he would get back in. He did. Apparently his mother had held strong and he believed he had no other choices. Despite his persistent anger and efforts to get me to react violently, I kept calm and called the Pemto Group Outpatient Center to see if the doctor was in and if we could stop by. Kevin hated Barry Lipsky and his verbal abuse toward me was getting closer to physical every minute. I said, "Let's just see what they have to say." Not getting a firm "No" answer, I headed immediately for the Pemto drug abuse center in Woodmere. Surprisingly, Kevin came in with me.

Barry recommended that Kevin go to a 90-120 day program in Jackson, Mississippi. Of course, Kevin adamantly refused. Then it was recommended that he go to the Karen Foundation for a 28 day program—cost $24,000 and they don't take insurance. This seemed cost prohibitive, especially considering that there was no guarantee that it would work. There didn't seem to be any good solution until Barry mentioned "Integrity Home" in upstate New York that would take my insurance and be reasonably priced in comparison. Kevin refused to go anyway but at least I had a plan to try to get him to agree.

I called Bill Greeley, my friend and assistant coach, to see if he would meet us at my place. I knew Kevin loved Bill and I needed a buffer. This idea must have come straight from Holy Spirit and led to a miracle breakthrough. With Kevin and Bill sitting on the couch together, Kevin's anger and resistance broke. Bill was able to convince Kevin that he had no better options than going to Integrity Home and living with his dad and Laura when he returned. It turned out to be a great night together for all of us. Matt came over with a bag packed by his mom and all the anger, hatred, and violence seemed to have dissipated into thin air. We told a lot of old funny stories and everything seemed to point to a breakthrough.

Kevin and I were going up to Integrity Home in South Fallsburg, NY the next morning.

Chapter 23 –
Integrity Home

⸺⬦⸺

The ride up to Integrity Home in South Fallsburg, NY took about two and a half hours. Kevin seemed relieved he was going to make the effort to clean up his act. He was in full confession mode about all the details of his life as an OC addict. Similar to the ride to his first inpatient treatment at SCCR when Joy was with us, Kevin was unburdening himself with all the secrets he had been forced to keep. With just the two of us in the car, Kevin confessed to virtually everything about his drug use including where, when, and how it began—and when and how the relapse happened. I was convinced there was a part of Kevin that really wanted to recover.

There seems to be an up side and a down side to being an opiate addict. Unquestionably, the up side is the feeling of peace that one gets when high on Oxycontin or heroin. Kevin described it as a feeling of total euphoria. It doesn't matter what you are doing or who you are with. It almost sounds like a substitute for reaching Heaven where one experiences only peace, joy, and love. The happiness he described when under the influence actually scared me because it sounded like he wouldn't trade the experience for anything; he absolutely loved the effect of the drug.

He also described the down side. His whole existence was based on getting the drug. Everything was about getting the money, scoring the drug, and getting high for 5-6 hours at a time. The rest of life got in his way a lot, however. Getting the money to get high every day requires a lot of effort and Kevin had to get it from his mother or me, or work for it, or steal it.

While at NU, he worked his mom and me pretty well for money until I caught on with his slip ups. Under the best of circumstances, working for money is difficult when going to college and playing ball on a scholarship. If you're addicted to OC, it is impossible. Stealing from strangers is dangerous and will eventually end with a loss of safety and freedom. Stealing from family and friends requires an enormous betrayal to those you love, but you're less likely to go to jail or be injured physically.

Not getting the drug is not an option once addicted. Getting dope sick from the withdrawals forces the addict to find a way to get the drug. As I said, Kevin's whole day revolved around getting the money, scoring the drug, and getting high. Eventually there was no room for anything or anyone else. He appeared to have lost all inner strength to do the right thing. An opiate addict will eventually lose everything and everyone who was ever important to him. But that will not stop him.

The idea of getting clean and getting a fresh start had a lot of appeal to Kevin on the ride up to Integrity Home. I felt closer to him than I had for a long time because of his honesty and I was hopeful that he wanted to end this nightmare once and for all.

When we arrived at the facility, it had a whole different vibe than at SCCR. It felt more like a vacation camp whereas SCCR felt more like a drug hospital. The people were friendly and upbeat; Kevin seemed encouraged and willing to turn his life around. After settling the finances and insurance information, I hugged Kevin goodbye and promised to come up to see him in about 10 days.

I received encouraging phone calls from him for a few minutes almost every night. He seemed to make friends easily and spoke highly of the program and the counselors. When Laura and I went up to see him on a Sunday, he looked terrific and seemed proud of himself. We all went to an AA meeting together—but somehow during that meeting Kevin changed. His facial expression and body language became sullen.

Following the meeting I asked Kevin what was troubling him. It seemed like a demon had entered his body and the friendly, upbeat kid had left. He said he would truly rather be an addict than go to AA meetings his whole life. He said there was no way he was never going to drink or smoke again and there was no way he was going to hang out with AA people for the rest of his life.

I was stunned. I thought everything was going great. Where did all this come from? We left Kevin for a while and returned to see him for dinner at the dining room. He seemed better and more relaxed. We went with him to meet his counselor, Rodney, and talked about Kevin's program for recovery. He was a young man with dreadlocks, maybe in his 20's, and he and Kevin seemed to like each other. Rodney spoke positively about Kevin's progress and asked us if we would come up on Wednesday for a 2-day family program. We eagerly agreed and we left Kevin that night, hopeful that he would lose his fear of living a life of sobriety.

Laura and I returned on Wednesday for the 2-day program. They gave us a nice room right there in the facility and we participated with a total of 23 people—10 alcoholic / addicts plus family members. The program was run by Tom Buchanan, a large, hard looking, sixty-one year old man. He was magnificent. I have a lot of respect for all the people whom I've met in the business of substance abuse treatment, but Tom Buchanan is my favorite. The morning program on the first day was very emotional with the addicts making a list of the things they had lost as a result of their substance abuse. The family members also participated in sharing their stories of what life has been like for them as a result of alcohol / drug addiction in their families. Listening to the stories of the broken lives, the fears, and the love that remains brought a great deal of raw emotional energy into the room.

I gained more and more of an understanding of what it is like to be an alcoholic / addict. I will never again believe that the addict just suffers from a bad attitude, a lack of self discipline, or any other character flaw. I realized better that they really suffer from a disease over which they have no control. The most fearful of them believed they would never be able to avoid relapsing when they got out of Integrity Home.

At lunch time, Kevin's fears erupted. He told me again he could not imagine a life of sobriety. Everyone he knows likes to party and there was no way he could live avoiding the drinking and drugging. He didn't plan on doing OC again but rejected totally the idea of a life of abstinence. The idea of not being able to hang out with his brother, his cousins, and his friends in the same social setting as always seemed out of the question. He was 21 and said, "This is just not going to happen."

He didn't want to finish the family program and said he would not return to the meeting room in the afternoon. And now he was angry because he knew how horrified I was to hear this. We seemed to be back at square one—and after all the big hopes we had that we were turning the corner after weeks of rehab. Kevin would not accept the premise that he had a disease. He didn't believe that if he did any intoxicants at all, he would most certainly find his way back to his drug of choice—Oxycontin. And if he was wrong about having the disease, he'd rather be a drug addict than a straight arrow living life at AA meetings.

Laura and I were obviously shaken by this. Laura was great, however, at helping me to stay calm. She reminded me that this was all part of the disease and that it would take more time for Kevin to accept it. She cautioned me not to react to every fluctuation in Kevin's attitude and to just stay the course, however long it takes. Laura's attitude strengthened me. After all, I was supposed to be the rock and she was supposed to be the one who got rattled by conflict. She was reacting great under pressure.

We went back for the afternoon session not expecting Kevin to show up. Kevin did come back but he sat on the opposite side of the room and refused eye contact with us. It was apparent to everyone there that something had happened between Kevin and me, so after the session Tom Buchanan set up a meeting for Kevin, Laura, and me to meet with him in his office.

Tom Buchanan had seen it all and been through it all as an alcoholic himself. He had a friendly, no nonsense approach to analyzing an addict's problem but, more importantly, had a presence about him that commanded respect. Kevin had said he was "the Man" and I was certain that he had Kevin's full attention. Tom seemed to recognize that there was a strong love between Kevin and me, so he took the soft approach. He pinned Kevin down on what it was that made him angry at his father. It came down to his fears about disappointing me by failing to become permanently clean and sober. Tom focused on the bond of love that the two of us shared and the strength that would provide in the long run.

Kevin melted in front of this big man. There was no anger left in him by the time the meeting ended. We all hugged and cried a little. Kevin was prepared to give it a try and we had a positive and meaningful experience together for the next 24 hours. As we said goodbye the next evening, we all had the intention of Kevin coming back to live with us in Long Beach. We had not resolved the issue of whether or not it was right for Kevin to return to NU in September to finish his degree. I knew I had to leave that up to Holy Spirit; it was not for me to decide without His help.

Days before Kevin was to complete his 28-day program at Integrity Home, I received a letter from him. He said he would try outpatient treatment and going to meetings but he still believed he could drink somewhere down the line. He admitted that he was scared of recovery, but strongly indicated that he did not want me to use the leverage of the car and the college tuition against him to force him into compliance anymore. He said it was important to understand that I couldn't control him and that I had to change my ways if we were going to get along.

As I look back at that now, what he was saying was the same advice that Holy Spirit had been giving me all along, but I didn't see it that way at all. I saw Kevin setting himself up for failure and dictating the rules to me. I called up Pemto and asked Barry Lipsky what he thought. He told me that Kevin was certainly not ready to be released from treatment with that attitude and that I should call Integrity Home and explain that Kevin needs more time. I called Kevin's counselor, Rodney, and explained my concerns. Kevin was due to be released the next day and I was asking for them to convince him to stay. Rodney called me back and asked if I could come up tomorrow and meet with him, Tom Buchanan, and Jim Cochran—the owner and founder of Integrity Home. Of course, I agreed and expected this to be the best opportunity to convince Kevin to stay.

Jim Cochran was probably in his 70's. As the founder of Integrity Home and a pioneer of drug treatment centers for more than 40 years, he had written a book about recovery that I had read and enjoyed. He, like Tom Buchanan, was another tough guy who was bound to gain the instant respect of Kevin, as well as myself. I met with Jim, Tom, and Rodney before Kevin came in. I explained the contents of the letter, the advice of Dr. Lipsky, and my fears about Kevin coming to live with Laura and me without an attitude of real dedication to the Twelve Steps and recovery in general.

When Kevin came into the meeting, Rodney explained my fears to Kevin. Kevin exploded in a rage at the perceived betrayal of me divulging the contents of his personal letter. He claimed that this was an ambush devised to keep him in rehab longer and it wasn't going to do any good. He adamantly refused to stay any longer and appealed to these rehab officials to straighten out his father on his controlling nature.

Jim Cochran tore into Kevin for his disrespectful attitude towards his father and his ingratitude for those who have sacrificed for him to have an opportunity to recover from a debilitating illness. He asked Kevin if he wanted to remain a hopeless addict and proclaimed that we had all been wasting our time and money if that was indeed the case.

Kevin quickly backed off his militancy and apologized to everyone there for his outbursts. Cochran and Buchanan didn't stand for any disrespect from addicts and had no problem dismissing anyone who wasn't interested in attaining recovery and a drug free life. Kevin's softened stance allowed them to hear his fears. They suggested that Kevin should stay longer and empathized with his personal doubts about recovery. After a while, however, they saw that Kevin was determined to leave and admitted that he was unlikely to gain anything from staying if he remained unwillingly.

The men asked me to leave the room while they talked to Kevin. Upon my return, the atmosphere in the room had changed to one of much less tension. The treatment officials admitted that Kevin was definitely in a challenging personal struggle; but he had completed the 28-day program, consented to outpatient treatment, unannounced drug screens, and 90 meetings in 90 days. It was decided that I would stay overnight and I would attend an AA meeting with the group that evening.

When we left the next morning, we were both of the belief that, although he faced a big challenge, he also had a chance of success. We made a vow: "No more deaths like John Bigelow." John was a great Sherwood athlete of mine from the early 90's who had recently died of a heroin overdose. We were returning to Long Beach for what would be a new living arrangement for Kevin, Laura, and me. I still can't say who among us felt the most anxiety.

Chapter 24 –
To What Voice Do I Listen?

It seemed as if the experiment with Kevin living with us never had a chance. Kevin didn't want to be controlled and if he lived with Laura and me, we would have a pretty good eye on his behavior. Kevin had attended an AA meeting up at Integrity on the morning we left. On the second night in Long Beach I recommended that Kevin should go to an NA (Narcotics Anonymous) meeting that was taking place only a few blocks away. Kevin resisted the idea right away and the conversation got contentious. Kevin had consented to the officials at Integrity Home that he would make an effort to attend 90 meetings in 90 days upon his release. This was day two and Kevin did not want to go.

After dinner I asked Kevin as gently as I could to please go to a meeting that night. I offered to drive him and pick him up, although it was a less than ten minute walk. Kevin finally consented to the gentle approach of my prodding and I dropped him off at St. James Episcopal Church. It took me about a minute to get home and Kevin arrived home 10 minutes later—with an attitude. He said when he went in, they were announcing people's sober anniversaries—1 week sober, 1 month sober, 6 months, 1 year. And everyone would clap and cheer for the alcoholic / addict's accomplishment. Kevin was so turned off by this ceremony that he walked out the back door within 3 minutes.

"This," he said, "is not what I'm going to do for the rest of my life. I won't do Oxycontin but I will not be hanging out with these people every night, I'm telling you right now." Kevin got into his car that I returned to him and said he was going to Merrick to visit his mom and brother. He later called and said that he wanted to stay there that night and would return to Long Beach in the morning. I talked to CB and she said there was no one drinking and that Kevin was welcomed to stay. She admitted that Kevin had a bad attitude about AA meetings, outpatient rehab, and the rules for recovery in general. We agreed to let him stay the night but I expressed reservations about this set up where he would run back to Merrick every time he didn't like something. CB said she understood but didn't know what to do about it.

****

I decided that only Holy Spirit could help me make the right moves because I felt ready to explode. This is the contemplation that I wrote in my journal:

Subject: *Kevin's recovery*

My thoughts: *Kevin walked out of an NA meeting and is reluctant to go to more. He is defiant now about his treatment—on day two of recovery. There seems to be no reason for him to be living with us if he doesn't go to meetings. By not going, he's setting himself up for failure. His refusal to try to heal himself is so frustrating. It's not part of the disease; it just seems to be a lack of inner strength—a fault in his character. I was about to give him the car so it couldn't be used as leverage—but he doesn't seem to deserve it. There just seems to be no reason to be with us if he's not going to treatment. My frustration is telling me to just cut him loose. Dr. Barry Lipsky says, "Parents never give up on their kids." I feel like giving up.*

> **Pray for Grace—followed by meditation**
> **Answer: "Your function here is forgiveness. Don't act so seriously about it. Take things more lightly. Kevin is a hard nut to crack. Stay vigilant, but don't judge**

or condemn him like you just did. Your function is forgiveness."

Question: *Specifically, what do I do with the car?*

My thoughts: *I planned on turning the car over to him and his mom's responsibility last January when he left SCCR. Kevin just never got it done with Motor Vehicle Department, and as a result, I had the leverage to get him into Integrity Home. By giving up the car, I get rid of an expense, headache, and possible future lawsuit. It removes one controlling aspect of my relationship yet it has been a key to the leverage aspect to control Kevin's treatment. This is a tough one. Please give me a definitive answer.*

Answer: "Keep the car until Kevin can afford to pay for insurance and repairs. Ask CB for help on Kevin and the car. CB needs to be included."

****

Within a week Kevin had moved back to Merrick without a word and was avoiding all contact with me. The source of his anger was that he wanted to return to NU against my wishes. The semester was starting in a week and Kevin wanted to get as far away from me and his life of sobriety as he could. I made the decision with the advice of the Pemto Group not to send him back. He saw me as his jailer again.

Laura cried heavily over Kevin's anger towards us. She tried so hard to be supportive of both Kevin and me, but nothing was working. There seemed to be a constant malaise in our life that was hard to shake. I hated putting her through this but saw no way around it.

I'd continue to turn to Holy Spirit for help and the message was consistent: **"Remain thankful for having Kevin as your son and for being allowed to participate in his recovery, no matter how bumpy the ride."** I was being reminded not to be offended by Kevin, nor to judge him for his behavior. If he could be any different—he would be.

His 22nd birthday was coming up in a week and I knew he dreaded it. I knew Kevin was actually in a personal hell and I truly believed he would need some kind of spiritual link to escape it. I believed that the Twelve Step program was his answer. It was obvious he was not ready yet and needed to suffer more. It was up to me to learn how to not suffer myself. I was not helping anyone by being devastated by all of it. My ACIM workbook lesson said, "Only my condemnation can injure me; only my forgiveness can set me free." I continued to ask Holy Spirit to help me lose all the condemnation that I felt for Kevin but to give me a role in his recovery.

Within a few weeks Kevin was back to using again. He doctored up his drug screens which didn't fool the Pemto outpatient clinic. Kevin accused the treatment center of looking for trouble and refused to return. He was angry, rude, and defiant. He wanted to take the car up to NU for Alumni Weekend. The lacrosse alumni were going to play against the current varsity team. Of course, a big party surrounded the whole affair.

The people at the Pemto Group were persistent about my using leverage with the car to get him back into treatment. Therefore, I told Kevin if he went to a meeting with me to resume treatment, I'd let him go to NU with the car. He went to the meeting but he was a nightmare with me and the staff. Everyone knew he was lying about everything, they were just interested in keeping him in treatment. They didn't care if he hated it, hated them, cursed at them, or anything else. They told me that if he's in treatment there is always a chance; if he's out of treatment, only bad things can happen. They assured me that those things can be very bad.

Again I had the same dilemma. The drug abuse experts tell me to use all force available to keep him in treatment. The Holy Spirit tells me to lighten up, love him anyway, don't condemn or judge, and realize that Kevin has to go through this. To whom do I listen? Experts in the field of drug addiction were unequivocal in saying to use all the force at my disposal or the consequences will be irreparable. I could not understand why God would put these dedicated and competent drug counselors in my life if I was not supposed to listen to them.

By December of 2005 it was time for me to decide if I would keep Kevin from returning to Northern University for another semester to get within easy striking distance of graduating. He only needed 18 credits and could possibly pick up 15 of those in one semester. I had made Kevin sign a contract back in September that if he was to go back to school, he needed three solid months of clean drug screens. That didn't happen. His mom wanted him to go back to school and at least accomplish something positive. She also needed a break from the stress of living with him.

****

As much as I respected the people at the Pemto Group, I felt I had to do what my Inner Guidance said. I recorded the following contemplation in my journal on December 12, 2005.

Question: *Do I go with my instincts and release Kevin and myself from the contract we established concerning drug treatment and total abstinence in return for going back to NU?*

My thoughts: *Recent messages from my spiritual sources indicate to me that Pemto's advice is not going to work with Kevin. I am using "force" and it is being met with a strong counterforce causing misery for everyone. My judgment of Kevin has been my biggest obstacle to peace and my biggest challenge to overcome on my path to a greater understanding. To let Kevin fulfill his karma—to not force him into anything—to pay his tuition and then let go of the results—seems to be the answer. Is this true?*

> ***Pray for grace—followed by meditation***
> ***Answer: "Write Pemto a letter saying that you appreciate their efforts, admire their dedication and motives, and that you've learned a great deal. Explain your feelings for leaving treatment and ask for their understanding. Meet with Kevin and release him from his contract. Kevin has***

problems but you can't heal him if he doesn't want to be healed."

Kevin's counselors at the Pemto Group pleaded with me to just meet with them one more time before we left treatment. I had been going to parent meetings one or two times a week for over a year with these counselors in order to learn everything I could. We knew each other well and they didn't want me to leave without one last meeting. They strongly urged me to bring CB and Kevin. They said they understood my thinking but virtually insisted we have one more meeting.

I had relied on these people at the Pemto Group for advice for so long that I felt guilty if I refused them one last meeting. I told CB and Kevin that if I was going to reject their advice and send Kevin back to NU, they would have to attend this meeting as well.

Nothing that the professionals from Pemto told me was untrue. They told me if I sent him back to college, his addiction would get worse. They told me he would say and promise anything that I wanted to hear, but would continue to use drugs at an accelerated pace. They said his lying and stealing would progress. They said his college education was unimportant until he was in a recovery program and had clean screens (drug tests) for a minimum of 6 months. They said this in front of Kevin and CB, both of whom wanted to get away from these people as quickly as possible.

I told all three counselors in the room that I didn't deny that they were telling the truth. I did not tell them or anyone else that the Holy Spirit had guided me to reject their advice. I just said that Kevin is not ready to hear anything that we have to say, so I'm sending him back to school to try and get something positive accomplished. They insisted that this was a dangerous choice that I was making.

Both Kevin and CB were happy that I did not let the drug counselors talk me out of letting him leave treatment and go back to school. It did make me happy to see Kevin smile and felt good to have him hug me and show honest appreciation. He acted as if a death sentence had been lifted. I also felt assured that whatever did happen as a result of this decision—good or bad—would be necessary in the big picture. I couldn't help but wonder what that big picture was going to look like.

Chapter 25 –
Love Him Anyway—And Let Go

Kevin returned to NU in late January and lived off campus in the town of Hadley in a big house with six other guys. Although I had anxiety about what might happen, things were much more peaceful with him away. He was appreciative of being allowed to return to school and I could hear love and kindness in his voice when I talked to him. This was a change from the previous year when I heard nothing but anger in his voice and felt bitterness in his heart. I knew he wasn't out of the woods as far as drug use went but prayed he wouldn't return to Oxycontin. I believed he had learned something from the two inpatient rehabs and the outpatient Pemto clinic. At least I knew I had learned a lot. Most important to me was that Kevin felt grateful—and gratitude is an emotion I had not seen from Kevin for a long time.

Having Kevin happy with his dad was also a relief for Laura. The constant tension from the previous year had put a strain on our marriage. Laura was supportive of all my efforts to help Kevin and she was particularly attentive to my mother, Phyllie, as her Alzheimer's progressed. It was Kevin's anger towards us when we were trying to help him that was most upsetting. Seeing my mom's increasing terror at not being able to remember where she was or what she was doing was truly heartbreaking. These were tough days and, although I couldn't have handled it as well without Laura's support, I couldn't help but wish that it would not have such an effect on her. For about three months we went through a period of relative calm. We did not have a lot of contact with Kevin. When we did, it was polite and easy.

At the end of April that changed. I received a phone call from Coach Randazzo that really shook us up. The coach got a phone call from the father of one of his players who lived in the house off campus with Kevin. The father knew me as the coach of Sherwood and I had spoken to him on several occasions at NU games. His son was a player of one of Sherwood's local rivals before joining with Kevin at NU. The dad told Coach Randazzo that he thought it was his duty to get me a message that my son was in deep trouble.

The son had told his father that Kevin Glenz was strung out on heroin with a friend named Hal up in one of the house bedrooms. The story was pretty sketchy from there. He said that one night Kevin was alternating between sweating and freezing and looked frighteningly pale after being in his room all night with Hal. Some of guys found needles and a spoon used for cooking up heroin in the waste basket. The father hoped he was doing me a favor by alerting Coach Randazzo, who he knew was a friend. Since Kevin was no longer a player on the team, he thought this was a good contact. He said to the coach, "If it were my son, I'd want to know."

Although I was embarrassed that someone in the lacrosse community would know the state of my son's drug abuse better than I did, I appreciated the effort to want to help. I decided to go up to his house in Hadley, unannounced, for a visit. Talking to Kevin over the phone would just bring about outrageous indignation from him and renewed accusations that his father was again causing unnecessary alarm. I felt it would be better to pop in on him with the report of what I was told.

Looking back, I should have consulted with the Holy Spirit first. It was my idea to sneak up and catch him by surprise but I guess the Holy Spirit must have had a different idea for as I was driving up—Kevin was driving down to Long Island. When I arrived at Kevin's house around 2PM, no one was in the house. Kevin's car wasn't parked in the back, so I figured he was at class. I sat in the back of the house for 4 hours before anyone showed up. No one knew where Kevin went. He didn't answer his cell phone when I called. I called CB and found out that Kevin was at her house in Merrick but he had already left. I told her the story about the parent's call to Coach Randazzo. Now she had been alerted that Kevin had probably relapsed on opiates—and the new word is "heroin" although it remains unconfirmed.

On the ride back down to Long Island, I was wondering why I was meant to take that long ride up and wait for 4 hours—for nothing. The thought entered my head that I didn't really hand that problem over to the Holy Spirit but had instead, taken things into my own hands to fix the problem.

It turned out that I never did get to see Kevin face to face to discuss the situation. He had returned to NU the next day. Whatever his mission had been on Long Island that had him drive up and back so quickly, it was never revealed to me. But now I felt I had to confront him on the phone about the accusations that had been reported to me.

As expected, Kevin raged in righteous indignation. "How could anybody say that?" "That kid's a bigger druggie than anyone." "They don't know what they're talking about?" "People are so fucked up, I can't believe it." On and on, the denials came. Then, as in the past, he switched his anger on to me again—and the old arguments were being replayed of my being a controlling, overbearing tyrant who overreacted to everything.

But I kept thinking of the ride home from the worthless trip to NU. I recognized that I was still trying to fix the problem, although Holy Spirit had said clearly to me many times to let his life unfold as it was meant to. I kept hearing, ***You don't know what Kevin needs to go through—so stand back.*** That was clearly Holy Spirit's advice—and I just wouldn't listen.

****

The same message kept coming anyway. Every day I would turn to Holy Spirit and be gently told, ***Focus on forgiveness, tolerance, and non-judgment.*** Doing that certainly didn't come naturally; and it was apparent that I did not yet have enough trust in Holy

Spirit's advice. Yet every day I would hand the problem over to Him and hear a similar response.

Kevin had returned home to Merrick but had received poor grades and failed a mandatory class that had potential to further derail his eventual graduation. Kevin was now a "social work" major in the area of sociology. To graduate, he still needed to take a mandatory course in summer school at NU. He had some technical obstacles to clear up, plus 6 more credits that he could take off campus at our local community college. He would not be going back to NU to live or go to school anymore.

Still, since his return home, he wasn't getting any of it done. I would get frustrated and when I turned to Holy Spirit, I would get, *"Love him anyway—and let go of it."* Nevertheless, on the occasions that I did see Kevin, I still left him feeling like he was inadequate and a disappointment. I couldn't let it go. I knew he was using.

In early July, I took 12 wonderful teenagers from Sherwood HS to Scandinavia for a few weeks as their group leader. As always, being away let me clear my mind and look from a different perspective. We cruised around the Baltic Sea—starting in Helsinki and on to Talinn, Stockholm, Copenhagan, Oslo, and to the fjords of Norway. It was still light out at 3AM and the sun never seemed to fully disappear. I felt that this trip was giving me the opportunity to see Kevin's situation through different eyes. I was convinced that my job was to love Kevin anyway—and let go of the results. Kevin provided great opportunities for me to learn to forgive—and I was told to take advantage of the opportunities.

In late September of 2005 it became confirmed that Kevin was again addicted to OC. But now, he was no longer a full time student—and so he was no longer covered by my health insurance. He had free room and board at his mom's house. She paid his car insurance, car repairs, and his cell phone. Kevin sporadically worked as a caddy at a golf course—but any money he made was gone instantly. And my giant change jar filled with nickels, dimes, and quarters suddenly was mysteriously low. Kevin had come through an open back door in our condo, up the stairs to my bedroom and stole about $30 of coins at a time. Once we found that out, we never left a door open again. Kevin was obviously desperate.

By Christmas of 2005, Phyllie was moved to a nursing home in Long Beach closer to me where Laura and I could keep a better watch on her. She needed a lot of help and a nursing home could provide it. We all went to my brother's house for Christmas. Phyllie had a good Christmas with us and both Kevin and Matt came over to visit. We ended the night meeting Matt and Kevin at the house of my best friend, Stevie T. I was grateful that Christmas went by without any incidents.

And we received good news that Kevin had completed the 6 credits at Nassau College and had now fulfilled his requirements for graduation from NU. For whatever that might hold for him in the future, Kevin had accomplished something while a drug addict. He was a college graduate of Northern University, earning a Bachelor of Arts degree in social work.

What would 2006 bring? I had a strong premonition by this time that things would get worse before they got better.

Chapter 26 –
2006

It was the 19th of January when I received the phone call from Joe Renken that Kevin was found unconscious from a heroin overdose in Brooklyn. As fate would have it, the father of one of Kevin's closet friends had died and the wake was the next day. The story of Kevin's overdose had spread quickly through the Sherwood community. When Kevin and I showed up at the wake, the buzz went through the crowd instantly. Both Kevin and I could tell from the people's reaction that they had heard about it. Kevin and I stayed pretty close to each other it seemed, so that we wouldn't get picked off one at a time and have to answer any questions about the overdose.

Kevin was remorseful about the overdose and wanted to go to an outpatient treatment center. First he said he would need something to help with the withdrawals. We went to my family doctor in Sherwood to see if he could prescribe something that would help Kevin. Certainly the doctor was surprised to find that the coach's son, the lacrosse hero, was a junkie. He gave Kevin a prescription for something mild and recommended the finest doctor around in the field of drug treatment, Dr. Barry Lipsky. I cringed because I knew Kevin would not want to return to the Pemto Group. He had already said that he wanted to pick out a treatment center by himself. But he had no money, no job, no insurance, and a big drug problem.

Kevin started to attend AA or NA meetings with his old NU "drug buddy gone clean"—Hal. Hal had devoted himself to the Twelve Steps since an intervention from his parents about a year earlier. Hal had been calling Kevin. He was saying things like, "Free yourself from slavery, Kevin. Recovery is better than addiction." Kevin seemed to like and respect Hal; and Hal was truly devoted to the Twelve Step program. I asked Kevin if he would give me Hal's cell phone so I could call him. He did and I set up a breakfast meeting with him at a local diner.

Hal was as cooperative as he could be. He was proud that he had freed himself from opiate addiction and was devoted to helping others. He would especially love to help his friend, but told me that it was totally up to Kevin. If he wanted it, there was help. If he didn't want to get clean, no program would help him. I asked him a few questions about his drug use and Kevin's. He promised to tell me everything I asked about his own drug use. The other information would have to come from Kevin. Hal spoke about the power of turning to his Higher Power. When I saw how strongly the program had affected him, I felt certain that the Twelve Steps would eventually be the spiritual program that would lead Kevin to a connection to his Higher Self. That didn't mean he was ready yet.

He attended AA meetings with Hal—but not for long. He started at an outpatient treatment center in Long Beach—but said it was too expensive. I knew this act from before. He was playing along like he was in a recovery program. It would get people off his back temporarily but I knew that—what I called "Rehab Lite"—wasn't going to work. He needed total devotion like I saw from Hal. This was a little willingness that he was giving—but not a commitment. But my job was to, ***"Forgive him and love him anyway."*** Holy Spirit had made this clear but . . . it was hard to follow.

****

Now that Kevin was home in the spring, he said he would like to help out my lacrosse team as a volunteer coach. He didn't make it to many practices and was a bit out of control at times on the sideline during games but I was glad to have a positive venue and experience that we could share together. Lacrosse had certainly provided that for us in the past, and hopefully would again. Even though I knew he was using, I wanted the chance to let him know that I loved him.

My mom, Phyllie, died unexpectedly in May. It was a blessing because she was in terror most of her waking hours from her dementia / Alzheimer's. She never did know about Kevin's drug problems. I was hoping she was joining my dad in Heaven watching over Kevin. For seven years, Kevin had been the first person Phyllie thought of when she awoke and the last person before she would sleep. When Kevin went off to college, she lost her function—and then her mind started failing rapidly. Kevin was affected by her death, even though he hadn't spent much time with her since he moved back with his mom in Merrick after high school. At one point after Phyllie's funeral, he turned to me and said, "Now you've only got me to worry about." He recognized the strain that watching my mom deteriorate was having on me. I told him that I wasn't worried about him—thinking of Holy Spirit's advice to me. But I was lying—and he knew it. I was scared.

****

I continued to strengthen my connection to Holy Spirit by handing over all my fears of Kevin to Him. Soon after Phyllie's funeral, I was awakened in the middle of the night with a feeling of urgency concerning Kevin's drug use. I felt I had to do something but I didn't want to go against Holy Spirit's advice. I wanted further assurance that I was doing the right thing. This was my contemplation at 4:44 AM on May 22, 2006.

Question: *What should I be doing now?*

My thoughts: *Now that Phyllie has died, I realize it is true what Kevin said to me to me at her funeral. "Now you've only got me to worry about." I told him that I don't worry about him, but that was a silly thing to say. It doesn't seem right that I should be doing nothing while Kevin continues his drug use and makes no progress toward a meaningful life. I firmly believe that I will be guided by Spirit to help Kevin when the time is right. That is why I'm here now—downstairs in the early morning on the day of a playoff game against Wantagh—because I was awakened* *by a sense of urgency about Kevin's problem. I am here to listen to Holy Spirit. What should I be doing now?*

> ***Pray for Grace—followed by meditation***
> ***Answer:** "The way you have been treating Kevin recently—with unconditional love as your intention—without intending to throw guilt at him over his lack of productivity—by being an example of someone he would want to emulate—IS THE RIGHT WAY! Be patient. This time for Kevin is crucial to eventually get him to a place where he asks for help—receives it—and heals. Patience is the key for you. You'll naturally want this to happen quickly but it won't happen that way. There will be more heartache with Kevin before he heals. God will **not** leave you comfortless during this period."*

****

A few weeks went by without much change and I continued to ask Holy Spirit to guide my moves. In early June I received this advice in my meditation.

> *"Use Kevin's friends now, if they'd show up. Continue to be patient, but show an active interest in finding a solution with those people who love him. That is your avenue to help."*

I was thrilled to get some direction to actually do something. I called several of Kevin's best friends and asked them to meet me at my place. I've known these kids (men) for years as their teacher, coach, and, of course, as Kevin's father. I decided not to invite the ones that had OC as a drug of choice. The guys willingly came and wanted to do whatever they could to help. These guys were big time partiers, but they weren't doing Oxycontin like Kevin—and they loved him. They confirmed that they suspected he was back on OC but he didn't confide in any of them. In fact, he would leave them in order to score some OCs—do them up with other guys—and then return to his friends all wasted. They knew exactly where Kevin was at the moment that we were talking. One of the guys made a call and found out Kevin was nodding out on the couch of a friend in the middle of a party—obviously wasted on Oxycontin.

I appreciated all the information that these guys were willing to provide. They admitted that they were obviously no angels themselves, but they knew that Kevin was in trouble and would do anything to help him. I'll always be grateful to them for coming to my house that night. There was a lot of love there and I'll never forget it.

****

A week later, Kevin got fired from his job where he was parking cars for a restaurant. He was furious at a female manager who was responsible for firing him. As usual, Kevin was projecting blame on to someone else. Kevin was upset and called me close to midnight and said he needed to come over to talk to me. In order not to wake up or upset Laura, I met him on the beach across from our condo.

We started walking along the shoreline going east and Kevin wanted to confess that he was badly addicted on Oxycontin but still had a major resistance to treatment programs. His words were, "I can see why people commit suicide, because you're damned if you do (i.e. continue drugs) and you're damned if you don't (i.e. go to rehab / life of sobriety)." As we continued along the beach for a few miles east, the conversation was calm and gentle. Kevin was sick of being a drug addict and bemoaned the belief that he'd always be one.

When we turned around to walk back west, the wind had picked up fiercely and was in our face. The conversation between us seemed to go the same way. A demon seemed to have entered Kevin's body. Behind his eyes was that blazing fire of hatred and violence that was suddenly coming at me. The two mile walk back was full of screaming about how screwed up all the treatment centers are and how he'll always wind up going back to drugs anyway, so there is no reason for me to waste the money. The fear that he had no choice but to do drugs was fixed in his mind. And now his anger and frustration were projected at me.

When we finally reached the part of the beach that was close to home, we both decided to stop talking and just sit on the boardwalk. We sat there next to each other for about an hour without saying anything at all. It was 3AM and we were alone facing the ocean. Finally, after this unusually long silence, we just hugged each other and left, promising to talk again tomorrow. Neither of us knew what to do.

We talked on the phone the next day and Kevin seemed serious about getting into a plan of recovery. He had no money, job, or insurance but he seemed more willing than before.

****

On 6/13/06 I did another contemplation with Holy Spirit.

Question: *Do I push Kevin to go to an inpatient recovery such as Integrity Home or allow him to direct his own recovery that he finds for himself?*

My thoughts: *Kevin looked good yesterday despite the withdrawals. He has lined up two appointments that deal with recovery. I've enlisted Bill Greeley for his support and I get the distinct feeling that I am to let Kevin take control of his own recovery process, as much as possible. My doubts about his perseverance in true recovery may be well founded; but it must be Kevin on his own that recovers. How much do I back off? How active should my role be now?*

> *Pray for grace—followed by meditation*
> **Answer: "Of course Kevin needs control over his own recovery. Don't push the inpatient 28-day programs now. He associates them with failure. Let the outpatient treatment lead him in whatever direction it goes. Perhaps inpatient treatment will come from it. Remember that this may not be the time he recovers but his ultimate recovery is certain. You must stay patient. More failure will come before success."**

****

Although I loved Holy Spirit telling me that eventually he would recover, I still didn't trust that. I had been clearly told to be patient and let him go through whatever he needed to. I just couldn't get myself to fully believe it. In meditations, Holy Spirit would say to me, ***What if you knew that he was going to be okay in the long run? Could you live with the addiction now if you absolutely knew he'd be okay down the line—that he'd be helping others and would become a productive member of society in the service of others? If you knew, could you live with it?***

I said to myself, "Absolutely. If I knew he'd be okay I could let go of all my fears and relax." There was no question that Holy Spirit was telling me in a variety of ways to be patient and just love him. The messages from Holy Spirit were so consistent, but I had not yet developed the trust necessary in the "Voice" that was coming to me. The Voice didn't have a sound to it; it was just my thoughts after I had handed them over to the Holy Spirit.

How was I to know that this was, indeed, the Voice of the Holy Spirit instead of my own ego playing spiritual tricks on me? How was I to develop the trust necessary to know that I was being guided by my Higher Power? The answer seemed to be in the way I felt when I was listening and receiving help from my Inner Guidance. If it was peaceful, gentle, and reassuring—it was Holy Spirit. If it had elements of fear, anger, anxiety, or any negative feeling—it was the ego.

But how is that trust in the Voice developed? The answer is simply—PRACTICE. The more often one hands over all concerns or problems to Holy Spirit, the more trust is developed. Practice has a cumulative effect. The more you do it, the stronger the belief gets. It's like lifting weights; you don't always have to enjoy it, but with consistent repetition the strength increases.

So I would ask, "How many times a day should I connect to the Holy Spirit?" ACIM is clear on that. I should make no decisions on my own. With vigilance, I can learn to turn to Holy Spirit in all my thoughts. I should make no decisions on my own. I have a Source that is infallible if I can develop the trust to turn to Him in all cases.

A better question is, "How many times each minute should I turn to Holy Spirit?"

I therefore realize that Kevin's drug addiction is leading me to forming a stronger connection with Holy Spirit. The worst part of my life was actually the part that was strengthening me the most. It was beginning to become clear that turning to Holy Spirit was the ONLY real function I had. If I did that, everything else would take care of itself.

In the Workbook of *A Course in Miracles,* Lesson 135 says:

> ***"What could you not accept, if you but knew that everything that happens, all events, past, present, and to come, are gently planned by One Whose only purpose is your good."***

I needed to trust that no matter the outcome, whatever happens will be for the greater good.

****

With Kevin going to outpatient treatment of his own choosing, we were getting along great. Kevin came over to dinner one night and we started watching a basketball movie *Glory Road* after we ate. When the movie was over Kevin and I started to talk about his drug use and recovery.

Although this was exactly what I wanted to talk about, the details of his drug usage started to upset Laura terribly. It was frightening, but I wanted to hear every small detail while he was in the mood to confess. We went out to the boardwalk where we could finish our conversation unabated.

Kevin's description of the thought process that led him to do drugs was fascinating. I knew Kevin had no real belief in a connection to his Higher Power, but I couldn't help but believe that would change in a program of recovery. I kept asking Kevin, "Where do you think the inner strength to be successful in recovery is going to come from?" His answer was always the same. "I don't know."

Some time, somehow, I knew I was going to make inroads to the message that he could choose God instead of drugs. I didn't know how or when this spirituality would reach him. I could tell him with conviction that choosing his Higher Power was where the "strength" was going to come from.

At that moment I felt certain that the Holy Spirit was going to work through me to bring him to this choice. I also knew at that moment that I could be certain of the final outcome. I remembered a quote from ACIM—*"Infinite patience brings immediate results."* At that moment I felt a strong trust.

****

As I did every July, I was taking a groupl of Sherwood HS kids on an educational tour—this time to England, Scotland, Wales, and Ireland. It just so happened that at the same time, CB was going to Florida. Kevin had been clean for three weeks and I asked him if he thought he'd be okay alone in the house. He said he would be, but he asked if I could give him some money to get by while we were both away. I didn't feel good about giving an addict cash, but since he was clean and I wanted to show that I trusted him, I gave him money.

When I returned from Europe, Kevin said that he was going to AA meetings and outpatient treatment. He got a job from a friend of ours working in construction cleaning up a demolition site. CB had gotten rid of his car a while back, but now felt that we should both contribute to get him a new one. Apparently Kevin had been using his mom's car and she wanted him to have his own. I was happy that Kevin was in treatment so his mom and I both contributed $2,000 each and got him a SUV in good condition. The car was in his own name and it was his responsibility.

Shortly after that Kevin stopped going to AA meetings and outpatient treatment. I had difficulty getting him to call me back. This wasn't a good sign.

****

As Kevin's 24th birthday came on September 1, I asked Holy Spirit's advice in a contemplation.

Question: *How do I deal with Kevin today on his birthday now that he has left treatment? Do I ask questions and give advice?*

My thoughts: *On Kevin's birthday last year, I decided to leave his addiction problem to himself and see where it led. It led to the use of the needle, a heroin overdose, OC addiction, and no decent job. His two month recovery effort with outpatient treatment and attendance at AA meetings showed an effort on his part—but he was never fully committed. Today I met him for the first time since we bought him a SUV. I have difficulty forgiving him for shunning me right after we gave him a car. I know he's filled with guilt over it and ready to project this on to others who judge or condemn him.*

> ***Pray for Grace—followed by meditation***
> **Answer: "Deep in your heart, you knew that the last effort at recovery would fail because he lacked a strong commitment. Nevertheless, you also knew it was a major step forward that he volunteered to get help. At 24, he's still not ready—but he does better understand his problem. He is still going to mess up and will have to live with the results. Your job is to still love him unconditionally, don't enable his drug addiction, and let Holy Spirit handle the details. Use this as a forgiveness opportunity every time you feel fear, anger, frustration, or anxiety. Remember all you have learned. This is a projection of your unconscious guilt. Forgive him, forgive him, forgive him—in the new way."**

I met Kevin for lunch the day after his birthday. I never mentioned drugs, treatment, his car, or money. As a result, we got along great and had a good lunch. This time, I silently forgave him and handed it all over to Holy Spirit. But I couldn't help but wonder, "Was this really a responsible way for a parent to act knowing as I did that he was using?" When we left, we hugged and smiled. I think we both appreciated the lack of drama. I was starting to trust the advice.

Kevin now had a beautiful girlfriend, Bridget, who was a former Sherwood history student of mine and a recent graduate of NYU. I couldn't help but wonder, "What was she doing with Kevin?" I found out that she didn't know anything of Kevin's problems. He met her in the two months he was clean and had successfully hidden his drug use since then. Still—Kevin had no money, no job, lived with his mom . . . really, what was she doing with him? Bridget had so much going for her—but she obviously didn't see Kevin the way I saw him (i.e. lost, desperate, troubled).

When a friend told her that Kevin had been to rehab for opiate addiction, she confronted Kevin with it. He admitted it and convinced her it was in the past. This was a smart, beautiful, and articulate young woman but as they say, "love is blind."

On Christmas night of 2006, Matthew and his girlfriend, Jillian, Kevin and Bridget, and Laura and I all met up at the house of our best friends, Stevie T and Rosey. Stevie T is Matt's godfather and we have shared Christmas together for many years. Because the boys spend much of the holidays with their mom and her family, I am very appreciative to see the boys at the end Christmas with our warm and generous friends, the Trentacoste family.

We were all drinking the potent homemade wine of Rosey's father, Mr. Pinto, and had a wonderful Christmas night together. It was easy to see why both sons of mine could not picture a life where drinking was not a big part of it. Drinking parties were always a huge part of our lives and asking all our friends and family to change that custom because of Kevin's addiction seemed impractical.

It certainly would be a lot easier if Kevin didn't suffer from the disease of addiction. It would have been easier if he was like other guys his age and just drink a little and / or smoke a little pot. But Kevin certainly did have a serious disease and, at this point, he just wished that he didn't.

Chapter 27 –
2007

It was January when I received a call from Bridget. Kevin's friend Jack actually told Bridget that he thought that Kevin was back on OC and encouraged her to call me. When I got the opportunity to meet both of my sons together at a local bar, I told Kevin that the word is out that he's back on OC. Kevin just looked at me, paused about 10 seconds, shook his head and then walked out. Kevin would continue to deny. So, as I learned to do, I handed the situation over to Holy Spirit and hoped it would work out as it was intended.

Because I believed that Kevin needed a strong connection to his Higher Power, I was disappointed with how he was turned off by the Twelve Steps. Although they (12 Steps) seemed a perfect avenue for Kevin's recovery, he was resistant. He'd say, "I don't believe in this Higher Power stuff and I can't fake it." Having been an agnostic myself for 30 years, I could understand. Nevertheless, without that inner strength that turning to your Higher Power provides, he won't make it. But my job wasn't to figure that out. My job was to love him unconditionally, not judge him. I've been told many times now by the Highest Source that I have no way of knowing what Kevin needs to go through. I needed to put my trust in my Higher Power and let go of the outcome. Letting go of the outcome is tough unless you trust your Inner Guidance.

****

I had become active in a global church based on the concepts of *A Course in Miracles*. *Pathways of Light* is located in Kiel, Wisconsin but has membership throughout North America and in parts of Europe, Latin America and Australia. The church offers courses that lead to ordination as a reverend. At the time, I wasn't much interested in being a reverend but I was interested in studying ACIM with others. I started taking the *Pathways of Light* courses and was assigned a facilitator with whom I worked over the phone in discussing the content. My goal in joining this spiritual community was to further strengthen my connection to my Higher Power.

I talked to Louis, my *Pathways of Light* facilitator, about Kevin's addiction. Louis had a lot of knowledge about opiate addiction and he was a great comfort to me. Louis suggested that I try an addiction psychologist for Kevin. Kevin was agreeable to the idea of seeing someone who would help him. Kevin admitted that he'd been on heroin, Oxycontin, or Vicodin every day for months. Since Kevin had no insurance, I willingly agreed to pay the $110 per 50 minute session.

The first meeting we attended together. Kevin seemed to like Dr. Garber. The doctor believed that he could get Kevin to stop using drugs through a series of breathing exercises that were designed to heal the anxiety that he believed was causing the addiction. Kevin stopped going after three appointments. He had no confidence in the methods of this psychologist and didn't want to waste my money.

Kevin could see no way out of his drug addiction. He was convinced that any effort at recovery was ultimately destined to fail. He said with conviction that a life as a drug addict was preferable to a life of sobriety. It was an obvious call for help, yet I was beginning to understand that I couldn't be the help he needed. I continued to talk to him about the Twelve Steps when he bemoaned the hopelessness of his circumstances. He knew the life of a drug addict was miserable—that he was forced to lie and steal from those he loves the most. He just didn't see an acceptable way out of it.

I also told Kevin about my *Pathways of Light* courses and explained to him that his addiction has strengthened my connection to the Holy Spirit. Kevin was in no way turned off by my passion for my spiritual path. In fact, he seemed to like the idea. I could tell that Kevin wanted that connection to his Creator but didn't see how to acquire it. Holy Spirit told me he wasn't ready yet. Holy Spirit never told me when or if he would be.

I practiced forgiving Kevin for his continuing addiction and forgiving his mother for enabling him. I threw a lot of guilt at CB but I was wrong to do so. She loved Kevin with all her heart yet she seemed to be a born enabler. She was doing what she felt was right. Projecting guilt on to her for Kevin's drug problem was wrong and I regret it. Because of my propensity to make her feel guilty, CB was never able to partner up with me to effectively help Kevin. She did the best she could. She did what she thought was right. I should have understood that and been more compassionate.

****

When July rolled around, Laura and I were off to France and Spain with 20 students on another educational tour. I was gone for a couple of weeks and upon my return, I found out that Kevin had a new source of revenue—forging checks. CB told me that he forged $700 of checks from her account while I was away. Apparently he had done this before but I had not been told.

I suggested that CB should have him arrested. His addiction was getting worse and he was going to commit more crimes if he wasn't stopped. CB could never get herself to put one of her sons in jail. I knew that but I still made her feel guilty for not doing it. Again I wrongfully put the blame on CB for Kevin's continuing addiction. I used her as a scapegoat to try and sooth my own frustrations. That never worked well and I regret doing it.

From watching an HBO special on addiction, Laura and I heard about the drug suboxone. There was some evidence that this was a wonder drug for curing opiate addicts. It supposedly calmed the cravings for the opiate and would make the addict sick if he took an opiate while on suboxone. The drug was expensive but it was worth a shot.

At first it seemed to work. CB said Kevin was not doing opiates and he seemed relatively calm and peaceful. She called it a "miracle drug." Within a few weeks, however, Kevin had sold the suboxone I bought him and stolen $400 more from CB. He had also opened up bank accounts and credit cards in his own name and somehow had gotten some money from them. Kevin didn't seem to care about any consequences. He was desperate to get a fix.

I didn't see how I could let this continue. Then I read something in one of my *Pathways* courses, *Adventures into the Sacred Life*, that said:

"How would we know how another's path is supposed to look? It may look to us like they are headed for big problems if they don't 'straighten out.' And chances are they might be taking a turn that will increase their pain and suffering. But how are they to learn if they are not offered the freedom to choose, just as Holy Spirit stepped back and wanted us to be ready to receive His help."

It continued on to warn me about interfering. It said:

"If we intervene, we may be delaying a person's coming to a turning point. For many a "crash and burn" experience has been what they needed to help them to let go and let God. Our part is to step back and remember the eternal truth about them."

Again I was clearly told to step back and let him go through whatever he needed to. I only needed to be vigilant about changing **my** mind about this situation and not be so concerned about making Kevin change **his** mind.

I continued to research rehabs on the internet and called several of them explaining Kevin's situation. The more I researched, the more I became convinced that a 4-6 month treatment program costing more than $30,000 was going to be in his future. I had heard stories of parents mortgaging their house to pay for such treatment and there was no guarantee of success. I learned that the chance of success was 5-12% for outpatient treatment. The longer the treatment, the higher the percentages rose but they still seemed discouraging to me.

A great teacher of *A Course in Miracles,* Ken Wapnick, wrote something that reminded me that Kevin was serving as my greatest spiritual teacher.

"A very difficult relationship—one that brings up a tremendous amount of anger, hurt, resentment, guilt, anxiety, etc.—then becomes a very powerful means, if we let it, for working through a huge chunk of guilt. For it is this deeply repressed guilt that has surfaced through the relationship."

In ACIM we are taught that we are not the victim of anyone. We make the world we see through projection of our own thoughts. We all have unconscious guilt that we have built up over the years or perhaps even lifetimes. It is through forgiveness, non-judgment, letting go and letting God that we learn to live in peace. We create our own personal hell by allowing negative thoughts to consume us. It has been said that holding grievances is like setting yourself on fire and hoping the guy that you're mad at dies of smoke inhalation.

Kevin, therefore, becomes my greatest forgiveness opportunity. He is my opportunity to "let go and let God." If I could get myself to remember that, I could do some effective parenting. It may be that simple, but it's certainly not easy.

At the end of July, I visited my parents' grave in Greenfield cemetery. Phyllie had joined my father a couple of months earlier and I was missing her. Their headstone is located right under a magnificent cherry tree in a setting of hundreds of different colored trees, bushes, and flowers. I brought a beach chair so I could sit in front of their names on the headstone for a while and see if they had any advice to give me. I had my journal with me, so I asked them a question: "What am I supposed to learn?" I meditated for almost an hour. When I was done I wrote the following in my journal:

"This is the greatest opportunity for personal growth that has ever been presented to me. I must always remember that, when dealing with Kevin, I must lose my frustration that I inevitably display when he doesn't buy into the recovery philosophy that I'm selling. It might be important for Kevin to be a drug addict for a longer time. Just seeing me write this makes me cringe. But if I knew that this was God's plan—that Kevin and all of us would have to endure what seems like unbearable

torment—because we all will emerge with an important, meaningful, valuable lesson that helps us and others— then God's Will be done."

I left the cemetery feeling stronger than ever before about handling whatever was to come. I thanked my mom and dad for the sagacious advice and promised to do my part. I asked them to stay with me always. I knew at that moment that they were the same as the Holy Spirit—always there just for the asking.

****

With the help of a friend of mine from Sherwood, Kevin landed a job in County Community Hospital working as a transporter. For the most part he transported patients in a wheelchair from one part of the hospital to another. I personally didn't think that I would like working in a hospital, but I was glad to see that Kevin really did. He talked about taking classes to become a radiology or MRI technician. Of course I couldn't help but think that he would be trying to steal opiates wherever he could find them—but I tried to remember that I was to let go and let God.

One of the advantages of working for the hospital was the medical plan it gave Kevin. With this outstanding medical plan, Kevin could get affordable treatment when he was ready. Unfortunately, Kevin didn't get around to activating his plan. I offered to go to the hospital with him to see if we could get that fixed. Kevin seemed incapable of getting anything done on his own. It was as if he was a child.

While we were there at the hospital, I asked Kevin why he doesn't now sign up for "Direct Deposit" of his pay check into his own checking account. It seemed juvenile for him to give his check to his mother and then have her give him money. I wanted him to grow up and control his own money in his own checking and savings accounts. Giving the check to his mom would put him into a perpetual childlike dependence and it leaves no record of where his money is going. But, again, I was trying to control Kevin's money situation—not letting go and letting God. I should have realized that drug addicts don't want or need a record of where their money goes.

One evening in October after a Sherwood High School football game, Kevin joined me and the coaches and our wives at Bill Greeley's house. Although they were aware of Kevin's problem and shocked at Kevin's pale, gaunt appearance, everyone was happy to see him and made him feel welcome. I hadn't seen Kevin so happy, actually joyous, in the company of Coach Greeley, Coach Stevens, and the rest of the football staff. While watching Kevin beam with happiness while all the coaches recalled old stories that included his days of playing football, wrestling, and lacrosse, I couldn't help feeling that the drugs had robbed him of everything he loved. But I also could see that the little middle school and high school kid that we all remembered so fondly was still in him somewhere—just waiting to be freed from the prison of drug addiction. When he left to all the hugs and positive well wishes from the coaches and wives, I had to walk away to the privacy of the side of the house to be alone. Although I was crying, I felt so much love was being sent to Kevin that God had to feel it too and send him the help he needed. There was so much love there—it just had to happen.

****

But it didn't. Kevin was good at only one thing now—getting the drug. He used to be an excellent athlete. That ended with his last lacrosse season in college. He used to be a conscientious student. That ended with the opiate use. He used to be a good son, a good brother, a good friend to many, but a heroin addict is completely self—centered and is focused only on one thing—finding a way to get the heroin and get high.

I guess you could also say he was good at hiding the effects of being a heroin addict. He fooled his girlfriend. He fooled his buddies. He fooled his family, but he couldn't fool them all forever. He would get caught in lies. He would get caught stealing from family or friends. He was always broke. He couldn't hold a job. He looked like a ghost. He hid the gross looking needle marks on his arms for a long time by always wearing long sleeve shirts.

Because of the needle marks, Kevin had to admit that he was mainlining heroin. Formerly he had snorted Oxycontin and sometimes heroin. Now heroin was cheaper and the needle was a much more effective delivery system—more bang for the buck.

Chapter 28 –
Love Kevin—No Matter What

S ince I was gentler with him and more compassionate about his problem at the end of 2007, Kevin was more revealing about his drug use. I asked him if he wanted to stop using. He said he really did but still didn't believe that going away to a rehab was the solution. We made an agreement to go to AA or NA meetings together. I decided to stop drinking completely so I could, in clear conscience, go to AA meetings with Kevin.

Our first meeting together was 2 days after New Year's Day at a local church. I picked Kevin up and he seemed excited about going with me. I was jubilant with his attitude. We sat together and listened to people speak about their addiction to alcohol and drugs. The speakers were dynamic and their stories were ones that inspired hope in others. I was so impressed with the love and support they showed for each other. There was a great camaraderie among the members. They were a bunch of characters, to be sure, with a load of personality. And I enjoyed their tales of the low points in their lives when they were out of control and powerless before the drug. Some had been in jail and others had been only steps away from death or suicide. Each of them found his Higher Power only after relapsing again and again. I learned that, in most cases, relapse was an important part of eventual recovery. This gave me great hope.

Kevin and I went out together to get coffee or ice cream after each meeting. This gave me a chance to see what he thought of each story and how it related to his addiction. I was pleased to see that he was in no way turned off by these meetings and these people as he once had been. I went with him twice a week to a meeting and he attended others with his friend Hal. Kevin and I even read from the "Big Book" of Alcoholics Anonymous together. I never realized that he was stoned on heroin in those moments.

After a few weeks I urged Kevin to get himself a sponsor and to establish a "home group". Having attended several AA and Al-Anon meetings each week, I knew that getting a sponsor was an important step in recovery. I was surprised that Kevin was resistant to that step. There seemed to be so many interesting guys that could have served as a sponsor for him. He said he would get a sponsor but didn't want to rush into it until he was sure of whom he thought would be good. Although that made little sense to me, I was conscious of the fact that this was his recovery—not mine. Kevin was stalling because he knew he wasn't serious about recovery.

Within a few weeks Kevin stopped attending meetings unless I went with him. I realized that was not a good sign. His motivation seemed to be to please me—not to recover from addiction to heroin. I would ask him if he was still using and he insisted that he had not done any heroin since the start of the New Year. When I asked him what drugs he was using, he would get uncomfortable, defensive, and evasive. Soon he started to call me at the last minute before meetings to give me an excuse for why he couldn't attend.

The Holy Spirit did not guarantee me success in getting Kevin clean and sober. He did guarantee me success in being able to handle anything that came my way—if I continued to turn to Him.

By the end of February things had gone bad again for Kevin. He lost his job at the hospital for sleeping on the job. As usual, he blamed one of his bosses for being unfair in his treatment of him. His appeal for reinstatement was denied by a superior. Again, he had no job, no money, no health insurance, and no car.

Soon after, his girlfriend, Bridget, found a bag of syringes in his room and realized that he was shooting up in the bathroom while they were together at night. Although she had been warned about his heroin use, she didn't believe it until she saw the needles and put it all together with his behavior. They had gone away on a trip to North

Carolina a week earlier. At the end of the trip, Kevin had run out of heroin and was a mess with dope sickness. Bridget hadn't realized what was causing this shocking change of behavior in Kevin at the time. Kevin drove home with her and two of her friends at 90 miles an hour. They were all afraid to talk to him or tell him to slow down because of the fury inside him. He looked like he was ready to kill someone. In the throes of heroin withdrawal, he might have—just by driving a car. Only an hour after Kevin got home to Merrick after dropping off Bridget, he called her and acted all cute and apologetic. He was like Jekyll and Hyde. She didn't realize at the time that the mood swings depended completely on the drug.

A week later when she found the syringes in Kevin's dresser drawer, she realized that her boyfriend really was a heroin junkie and she disappeared from his life.

****

Now he had no job, no money, no health insurance, no car, and no girlfriend. He had his mom's house to stay in, his mom's food to eat, his mom's car to drive when available, and his cell phone that his mom paid for. Kevin still needed to find a way to finance his habit. CB complained to me that he was forging checks from her account. I believed that he was destined to go to jail soon because he was going to commit crimes to get money for a fix. That's what heroin addicts do. They have to get a fix somehow and they are totally focused on that one outcome. Each day is devoted to that single pursuit.

Since my message from Holy Spirit had clearly and repetitively told me not to judge Kevin for what he was doing, I became more and more laid back as the father of a heroin addict. I offered to go to meetings with him if he was willing to keep trying. I offered to let him come down to help me coach lacrosse whenever he felt he wanted to keep that connection. Sherwood lacrosse was a mutual love of ours and I wanted to use anything available to keep a connection to him. Being kind and nonjudgmental toward him drew him to me. He needed help and I was the strongest, most positive figure in his life. I wasn't enabling him. I gave him no money or financial support at all and he didn't steal from me. I told him I would always love him but would not bail him out of jail if or when the time came.

****

While my son, Kevin, battled with his addiction, I became a *Pathways of Light* ordained minister.

Pathways of Light is a church without walls. There is a beautiful campus on a lake in the woods of Kiel, Wisconsin where people come for workshops or just to spend quiet time to be with nature and connect to their Inner Guidance.

I had been studying ACIM for twelve years by myself without any guidance except the Holy Spirit. There were some ACIM study groups in the area, but I had never sought them out. I received a catalog in the mail from *Pathways* and wanted to further my study of ACIM. I had no desire to become an ordained minister but I did want to take courses with other people who were interested in this spiritual path.

Each course had worksheets to answer questions, study materials to read, guided meditations, and processes designed to change one's thinking about the world. I was assigned a facilitator who was a *Pathways of Light* minister. Louis and I spoke by phone every Sunday morning for about an hour.

Louis is a psychologist in New York City by profession and had a soothing voice and manner. He is also an avid student of *A Course in Miracles* and I had so many questions from all my years of self study. Talking to another person who loved ACIM was wonderful for me. I was always disappointed if one of us had to cancel or postpone a Sunday morning conversation.

Pathways has over 200 ministers from around the world. It uses teleconferences to bring its entire people together from as far away as Australia. *Pathways of Light* is a different kind of church with a different kind of ministry. As it explains in its mission statement, "We are dedicated to joining with people around the world in awakening to the Love and peace of God within us all."

I have a passion for studying and sharing the principles of ACIM with others. Becoming a minister for *Pathways* has provided that opportunity. I don't know where this will take me. My mission is to strengthen my connection to the Holy Spirit and to help others to do the same. I no longer wanted to be a teacher of history. If God had a plan for me to teach *A Course in Miracles* or just to teach people how to turn to their Higher Power for inner guidance—I would be enthusiastic and willing.

****

The more I went to Al-Anon meetings, the more I felt that there might be some kind of calling for me in helping others with family members who are addicts. The teachings of *A Course in Miracles* and the Twelve Steps of Alcoholics Anonymous harmonized well for me. I had no idea what the future would hold for me but I was determined to leave it all in God's capable hands.

Meanwhile I practiced every day by handing Kevin's drug problem over to the Holy Spirit. My morning meditations always gave me the message.

> **"Love Kevin anyway—no matter what. He needs to go through this now. Offer help but don't pass judgment on him."**

Different forms of this same message had been coming to me for years, yet I still had trouble following Holy Spirit's simple advice. I wanted to trust that Holy Spirit could not steer me wrong but when Kevin started forging checks from his brother's bank account, I just about hit the roof. Kevin had picked up some of his brother's mail from the bank that had checks in it. Matt had moved out of his mother's house but much of his mail still went there. Matt worked at Citibank and was quickly able to trace where the money from his account had gone. When he found out that it was Kevin who had intercepted his mail and forged checks, he was ready to disown his brother and put him in jail where he belonged. Of course, Kevin provided an unconvincing story about just borrowing the money for a short time and planning to return it to the account before his brother ever knew he borrowed it. Even though the story made no sense, it pacified Matt as soon as the money was returned.

It was apparent that Kevin was desperate for cash. He did, however, have several advantages that would make acquiring the drug easier. First, he had access to his mother's car. CB took the Long Island Railroad into Manhattan every day to teach high school health and physical education. Kevin had the car all day. Second, Kevin had the connection to the best heroin at the best price. The dealer from Queens did not want a lot of white boys from Long Island visiting his home in a predominantly black neighborhood, thereby raising suspicion. Kevin could serve as an intermediary and earn himself some free heroin. Third, the drug dealer did not have a car, so Kevin could drive him to his clients to deliver whenever necessary—again earning some free samples for his services. I've never gotten a definitive answer as to how much money per day Kevin spent on his drug habit. Statistics say $150-$200 a day is normal, but it seems impossible that Kevin could maintain that cost for even a short time.

****

Chapter 29 –
Retiring from Sherwood

The spring of 2008 was to be my last as the head varsity lacrosse coach of Sherwood. Although I knew Kevin was using, I did not know to what extent nor did I plan to pursue an answer to that. I encouraged Kevin to come to lacrosse practice and games because I would not see him otherwise. He came mostly to games because they were more exciting. He stood next to me throughout the game with his normal mood swings from joy to anger depending on the circumstances.

I would usually ask him if he wanted to go for something to eat after the game and most often he did. By not pressing the issue of recovery, he was more likely to bring up the situation himself. We continued to go to AA meetings occasionally but I knew it was really just to appease me. I didn't force the issue upon him although he knew that I was focused on his drug problem whether or not I spoke about it. Lacrosse was the vehicle to bring us together and I did not want to lose my connection to him by badgering him about rehab and recovery all the time.

My last season as head coach had an impressive 14-2 record. Unfortunately, we were upset early in the playoffs. That brought my 36 year career to a sudden end. A few days later, CB called me to tell me that Kevin had stolen all her jewelry—including her diamond engagement ring—and pawned it for quick cash. Although Kevin denied it, she found some of the jewelry in the local pawn shops—but not the diamond ring.

I had been advised by my Higher Power not to judge Kevin by his behavior. Pawning your mother's wedding rings for drug money just seemed to be inexcusable. After a long interrogation, I finally got Kevin to admit to the theft but he swore that he never saw the diamond. It turned out that he had a partner—a heroin buddy who helped him evaluate the worth of the jewels. CB and I believe that the partner probably stole the diamond without Kevin's knowledge. There was never any way to tell the truth of anything that he was saying. I became convinced that Kevin didn't know when he was lying and when he was telling the truth.

I encouraged CB to bring the cops in on this. She didn't want her son to go to jail or have a record. I believed at the time that Kevin's only chance to get clean would be incarceration. His mother refused to take that step, believing it would follow him the rest of his life. Kevin was more desperate every day. Heroin addicts can't take a day off. The withdrawals start after about 12 hours from the last injection. By the second day the addict can start to suffer from muscle pains, stomach cramps, diarrhea, vomiting, cold sweats, and intense irritability. Days three and four are the worst withdrawals By that time, the addict would do almost anything to get a fix. Most heroin addicts wind up in jail because of crimes they commit to get the money they need to avoid these terrible withdrawal symptoms.

Because I managed to stay calm and mostly nonjudgmental with Kevin at this stage of his drug abuse, he turned to me in June and said he needed help. He was more addicted than ever before and couldn't keep the habit going without constantly stealing money. He wouldn't share with me who he stole from or how he stole but he admitted that he was in trouble and needed to get clean.

We checked what was available to addicts with no insurance or money. Nassau County Medical Center offered help. We waited in the emergency room all day for several days and no beds opened up in their detox program. They suggested that he try Flushing Hospital in Queens. We called there and they said they did have a bed available. I drove Kevin to Flushing and after he had filled out the paper work we shared a tearful and loving hug. I told him this was the beginning to a whole new life. Once he was detoxed we could try another inpatient rehab program; probably he would return to Integrity Home.

As I left the hospital I said a prayer. I asked God to give him the strength to beat this horrible addiction. The answer I received was, "**When he's ready!**"

****

Three days later was my retirement dinner. My colleagues from Sherwood HS and my wife, Laura, had arranged a gala affair in my honor. It was in the form of a "roast" and about 20 speakers told many hilarious stories about just how clueless and incompetent I am in so many areas of life. It was all in fun and about 200 people paid $75 each to attend on a Monday night. The room was filled with the love of my family, my friends, my colleagues, my former students and players, rival coaches, referees, and wonderful people from all different parts of my 36 years as a teacher and coach. Even my college lacrosse coach, Jack Eagle, traveled over 6 hours just to tell embarrassing stories about me from when I was a college player. It was certainly one of the greatest nights of my life and I was honored and extremely grateful to be on the receiving end of so much love.

The day before this grand affair, I had received a call from Kevin in Flushing Hospital. He told me he wanted me to come and pick him up because this wasn't doing him any good. I knew that he was certainly going through withdrawals and greatly encouraged him to hang in there. He flew into a rage and demanded that I pick him up or he would walk out of the hospital on his own. When I refused and pleaded with him to give it a chance to work, he screamed, "NO WAY!" and hung up the phone.

I didn't believe he would do it, but he did. He walked out of the hospital and got one of his heroin addicted friends to pick him up and get him fixed. I called Kevin's mom to tell her that he would be showing up at her door and encouraged her not to let him stay there. She agreed—and when Kevin called she told him he was not welcomed to stay there.

So on the big night of my retirement roast, I had no idea where Kevin was. It was natural for people at the event to ask about him.

After all, he was my son and a big part of my life as a Sherwood HS teacher and coach. He was the coach's son who helped lead us to two NY State lacrosse championships. Everyone who attended the dinner knew who Kevin was. Not everyone knew that he was a junkie and was in no shape to attend. Ironically he, more than anyone else I know, would have loved that night.

He knew about the dinner, of course, so I was wondering if he might still show up. His brother Matt probably had to answer more questions about Kevin's absence than I did. Part of me was hoping he would appear and part of me did not want him there at all. I knew how much Kevin loved me and I've always known how proud he was of my coaching achievements. However, he was fully occupied trying to get money for a fix and never considered anything else that night.

A few days later, Laura and I flew out to Colorado Springs for my induction into the National High School Athletic Coaches Association Hall of Fame. My athletic director, district superintendent, school principal, assistant coach, and others wrote flattering compliments about me and, as a result of their efforts, I was chosen as the New York representative in the prestigious Hall of Fame. The school district was generous in giving me the time away from grading final exams and paid for all expenses.

When it was my turn to be inducted, they gave a short biography which included mentioning my family. Surprisingly, they announced that I had one son, Matthew—and inexplicably left out Kevin. At that moment, I didn't hear another word from the emcee about my accomplishments. I had an eerie feeling that something terrible had happened to Kevin. I was being given the highest honor in the nation for high school coaches—yet my mind turned to Kevin's addiction.

I returned to New York to find that Kevin was back in his mom's house. Although I was upset that CB was still enabling him, I was happily relieved that my intuition was wrong and nothing terrible had happened to him while I was away. CB said that she found Kevin sleeping in the garage. He looked awful and his mother took pity on him and allowed him back in. She was in no mood to hear my opinion of her further enabling him so he could continue using. I was frustrated and said some nasty remarks that were meant to make her feel guilty. I finished by saying, "I want nothing to do with either of you. You two deserve each other. I'm out. You guys are on your own from here on."

I had one week left of school. While I made every effort to enjoy the last days of a rewarding career, I now had no contact with Kevin or his mom. I tried to find out from Matt what I could about the situation. Matt wasn't living there and didn't know much. By attacking CB, I felt that I had blown my opportunity to be of any help. I didn't want to be left out of the loop now. I had invested far too much in this to quit or give up.

I was scheduled to go on a trip to Greece the week after school ended. I knew I had screwed up again with CB and wanted to see if I could make amends before I left. Laura had given me a copy of the book, _Beautiful Boy_ by David Sheff. It is a book of hope about a father and his addicted son. I had recently finished the book and decided to put it in CB's mailbox with a note of apology. I told her I needed to be part of the solution—not part of the problem.

CB was touched by my gesture and invited me over to meet with her family that was in from Iowa, Florida, and Vermont. I was grateful that I was no longer going to be shut out. I realized during that week that attacking anyone because of my frustration was totally non-productive. I made up my mind then to never attack CB again and vowed to myself to make the most out of this restored opportunity.

****

Chapter 30 –
Iowa For Recovery

I am convinced that when one puts Holy Spirit totally in charge of any situation, it opens a path to a miracle.

Robert Brewer is CB's 41 year old second cousin from Iowa. When the terrible floods hit Iowa in the summer of 2008, much of Rob's property was damaged and his mom's house and all her belongings were destroyed. Before the floods receded, Rob decided to get away and bring his wife Marla to New York for a reunion with his large extended family. His aunts, uncles, cousins, nieces, and nephews were coming from Vermont, West Virginia, and Florida. The flood in Iowa had been devastating and Rob and Marla needed a break. Even more, they needed the love and laughs of a big family reunion. Rob particularly loves the ocean at Long Beach and rides the waves, body surfing for hours at a time.

My relationship with Rob goes back to his days as a teenager when he was having great difficulty with his step father in Iowa and needed to get away. Rob's mother, Kathleen, asked CB back in 1984 if Rob could come and live with us in Merrick to protect him from the violence of her second husband. Rob was only 17 at the time and CB and I agreed to have him live with us and our two boys. Rob lived as a member of our family and attended Webster HS in Merrick. He was like a big brother to Matt and Kevin. Little did I know that in taking Rob in, I was "paying it forward".

Rob grew up to be an impressive man. When he graduated high school, he went into the US Marine Corps and served as an embassy guard in Africa and other places around the globe. Upon returning to Iowa after completing his service, Rob married his beautiful wife Marla. Rob was always appreciative of the help he was given by our family in New York and loved to visit. He especially loved to see his cousins, my sons Matt and Kevin, whom he lived with for that year back in the mid 1980's.

When Rob found out about the situation of Kevin's heroin addiction, his immediate instinct was to help. Kevin was at rock bottom. He was terribly addicted, broke, jobless, and committing crimes (and getting away with them) to feed his habit. Rob and Marla offered to take Kevin back to Iowa to help him. Rob knew nothing about drug addiction.

Because CB had invited me over to see the family after I gave her the book, *Beautiful Boy*, I had the opportunity to talk to Rob. I said to Rob that it was, indeed, a generous offer to ask Kevin to come to Iowa, but it would be total insanity for him to bring a heroin addict into his home. I explained that first Kevin needed to be detoxed from heroin. Then he would need a minimum of a 28-day rehab program, followed by 30 AA or NA meetings in 30 days. He would need to be in a program of recovery for the rest of his life. Just going to Iowa wasn't going to solve anything for Kevin, but it could do damage to Rob's marriage and household. Kevin would steal anything and everything from them to get a fix if he was not totally committed to recovery.

Surprisingly, that did not intimidate Rob and Marla. Rob said that there were good drug rehab centers in Iowa and promised to make sure Kevin was in recovery and drug and alcohol free if he lived with them. Rob was in the position and of the nature to provide the discipline that Kevin would need to commit to recovery. Kevin had been away to rehabs before—each time he returned to his New York home where all his triggers were. Living in Iowa would be a truly fresh start. If he wanted to find drugs in Iowa, nothing could stop him. If he wanted to stay clean, Iowa had none of the triggers that led to relapse like New York did.

Rob offered this opportunity to Kevin. Kevin, surprisingly, accepted. Rob was an ex-Marine and he let Kevin know that there would be no half measures taken or allowed if he came with him to Iowa. After his 28-day program was completed, he would help Kevin get a job and Kevin would help Rob with the difficult job of the flood clean up that destroyed his mother's property.

As I was leaving for my annual summer educational tour—this time to Greece—the plan was for Kevin to go to Iowa with Rob and Marla and immediately begin a drug recovery program. When I returned from Greece I found that was exactly what had happened. Rob got Kevin an Iowa driver's license shortly after arrival, making Kevin an official Iowa resident living in Rob and Marla's house. And the state of Iowa would pick up 95% of the cost of the drug rehabilitation program.

I had believed for a while that we were missing the ingredients for a successful recovery for Kevin. I could get him detoxed and into rehab. Once he returned to either CB's house or mine he would be tempted by his lifelong friends to party. Once he drank or smoked pot—even moderately—it would only be a matter of time before he found his way back to his drug of choice. Kevin needed the commitment of 100% abstinence, and that had proved difficult in New York. Iowa was, indeed, a fresh start with none of the triggers that previously led to relapse. And Kevin would have an ex-Marine who would love him and watch him like a hawk.

****

I spent a lot of time meditating on Kevin's situation while in Greece. I did an amazing exercise that I saw in the appendix of <u>Take Me to Truth: Undoing the Ego</u> by Nouk Sanchez and Tomas Viera. The exercise comes from Byron Katie and is called *"The Work"*. It made me focus on my judgment of Kevin and helped to open my eyes about my inability to let things unfold according to a Greater Plan that is not mine.

When I returned home, I called Rob in Iowa and found to my joy that Kevin was indeed in rehab and had been detoxed. Kevin had tried to talk Rob into letting him come out of inpatient treatment after a few days and go to outpatient. Rob firmly refused. He told Kevin he could walk out of the rehab and go back to New York, but if he wanted to stay in his house, he had to finish the 28-day program.

Rob visited Kevin twice a week and participated in a family session with counselors and addicts on a third day. Rob was steadfast in his efforts to help Kevin and determined to provide everything that Kevin would need to make the transition to life in Iowa.

He set up his basement so that Kevin would have his own room, TV, refrigerator, and bathroom. He bought a good used car so that Kevin would be mobile and have some independence. He signed up for Direct TV so Kevin could watch his favorite New York sports teams—the Yankees and the Giants. He even found a local college lacrosse team—Palmer Chiropractic College—that needed a coach. Rob wanted this to work and made every effort possible to help Kevin.

I had the opportunity to speak with Kevin while he was in the rehab in Iowa called Country Forest. He sounded good. What seemed to make the biggest impression on me was the respect and admiration he had for Rob. That seemed to be of great significance if this effort at recovery was going to work. He told me that he could accept the first of the Twelve Steps—that he was powerless over heroin and that his life had become unmanageable. It was the second step where he was stalled—"Came to believe that a power greater than myself could restore me to sanity." He didn't feel that. I knew nothing that I could do could make that happen, but I planned on serving as an example of someone who gains strength from turning all decisions over to my Higher Power.

****

My uncle Gilbert, died at age 92 and his funeral in Decatur, IL was to be only a few hours' drive from Davenport, Iowa, where Kevin was to be released from rehab—coincidentally the day after the funeral. This synchronicity was not lost on me for a moment. I realized that I was meant to be both at my uncle's funeral and Kevin's completion of his 28-day program.

After arriving at the airport and renting a car to drive to Decatur, I called Laura to tell her that I arrived safely. She told me that I had just received a letter from Kevin. I asked her to open it and read it to me. As she read the letter, tears of happiness rolled down my face. It read:

Dear Dad, I'm sure you are wondering everyday how I'm doing. I can honestly tell you I'm doing real good. I'm really trying to work on myself and I'm not just talking about quitting drugs. That is a big part of what I'm working on, but I'm trying not to always take the easy way out—which is something I've been doing for the last eight plus years of my life. What they say is true—no pain, no gain—and that's the reality I'm facing. I still get impulses to quit and go home and do it my way. In the long run, I know where that will take me. I'm trying to play out the big picture in my head at all times. I'm not saying it's going to be easy, but either is being a drug addict. I know through recovery life will get better with time. One thing I promise you is I'm going to give it 100%. I wouldn't have come to Iowa if I didn't want to change. I still have daily cravings but they say that gets better with time. Rome wasn't built in a day and I won't get recovered in a day. But I'm excited about what the future holds for me. I think about you every day and I'm excited about rebuilding the great relationship we used to have. At times I feel very guilty about what I have put you through, considering what a great father you have been to me. I hear about all these people who didn't have dads or who had dads who were not around and I feel so lucky to have a dad like you. I'm not saying that recovery won't be a struggle; but I can honestly say my attitude on recovery has done a 180. I'm tired of being a boy, but I know being a real man takes commitment and discipline. Sometimes I forget how lucky I really am. I would love to have the peace I see in you and I know the 12 steps is the key to that peace. For now it's a struggle, but my heart is truly into it—no bullshit. I do miss NY but I know it isn't going anywhere. I promise I won't rush it. Love you always. Your son, Kevin

Laura faxed the letter to the hotel and I spent hours thinking about it and giving thanks to God for the way it made me feel. I knew that Kevin wasn't out of the woods as far as drug addiction went—and that he might never be fully recovered. I felt Kevin's love for me in that letter and I knew that love was all that really mattered. I stayed up most of the night just thinking about that.

After my uncle's funeral, I drove my rented car to Davenport, Iowa where Kevin was due to be released from the Country Forest Alcohol and Drug Rehabilitation Center. His cousin Rob and I got to attend his last group meeting the night before his release. The counselor was a beautiful young woman who, herself, had been a drug addict years earlier. The people in the group all got a big kick out of my New York accent—the same as they did over the last month with Kevin's.

The point that stuck most vividly in my mind from that meeting was the counselor saying that a change of venue doesn't make any difference to an addict. If the addict wants to use, there will be a way to acquire the drug. There are fewer triggers for Kevin in Iowa than in New York. Without a full commitment to the program of recovery, the addict will most likely find his way back to his drug of choice.

Kevin needed to go to 30 in 30—that is, 30 AA or NA meetings in 30 days. He would need to get a sponsor and a home group. He would need to devote himself to the Twelve-Step Program of Alcoholics Anonymous. Without this commitment, long term recovery is unlikely.

When we picked up Kevin the next day, we were all joyous at the situation. Kevin looked terrific. He had gained about 15 pounds over the last month and looked handsome, happy, and healthy. Kevin took a while to say goodbye to the people there, counselors and patients. It was easy to see that Kevin was extremely popular with everyone at Country Forest. Being a young man from New York, he was somewhat of a novelty and was a big hit with the guys—perhaps even more with the ladies. Kevin is a charmer for sure.

Since there was an AA meeting at Country Forest later that night, Kevin returned hours later to what looked like a hero's welcome. I was proud that he had made such a positive impression on so many people during his 28 days at Country Forest and truly enjoyed all the smiles and pats on the back that he received from them. He also seemed to feel good about himself. He was excited about getting a fresh start in Iowa and looked forward to getting a job so he could start paying his way at Rob's house and start paying back his mom and me for the debts we were covering for him. Making amends to those you have harmed (Step 9) is an essential part of the recovery process.

I was staying at a local hotel, so Kevin stayed with me for the first three nights of his recovery before moving in with Rob and Marla. We stayed up talking most of the night about everything from his life of drug abuse to family stories we recalled from over the years. We were both happier than we had been in many years together. I really wished I could have stayed with him in Iowa. He looked so good and so happy.

Rob and I went to get him a cell phone so I could stay in close touch with him. Rob had made plans to take Kevin sky diving the next weekend and to a Yankee-Twins baseball game in Minnesota the following week. Kevin even met with the lacrosse team from Palmer College while I was there and started teaching them how the game should be played. Lacrosse teams are uncommon in Iowa and Kevin's background in the sport certainly made him an expert for that region of the country. Kevin was actually a college lacrosse coach. Amazing!

It was a miracle. Just a month earlier, there seemed to be such little hope and now there was such an incredible opportunity for a successful recovery. Because there was so much love coming from everybody and from everywhere, I thought my heart would burst open from all the joy that was filling it. I gave such enormous gratitude to my Higher Power for allowing this into my life. I knew there were no guarantees, yet I liked the chances.

Chapter 31 –
Thanksgiving 2008

When I returned to New York from Iowa I had great faith that something monumental was happening in Kevin's life. He was getting a fresh start and was showing a changed attitude. In speaking with him several times a week, Kevin seemed to be happy. He admitted that he still had the cravings and was resentful that he had this disease. He wished he could be normal like everyone else but he recognized that he wasn't. He needed to totally dedicate himself to recovery if it was to work.

Laura and I made plans to go out to Iowa and celebrate Thanksgiving with Kevin, Rob, and Marla. Ironically, after we made the arrangements to fly to Iowa, Kevin called and said he was coming back to New York for a few days to settle some financial matters with Flushing Hospital over a bill for about $4,000 that he was charged from his two day failed attempt at detox back in June. The hospital told Kevin that if he came in person, presented his case, and signed the proper forms—his fee would be substantially reduced. Kevin had the ability to fly stand-by for free because of his uncle Larry who worked for American Airlines. I was nervous about Kevin returning to New York so soon. All the triggers were here. Anyway, there is no way I could forbid it. Plus it was financially important to reduce that big bill from Flushing Hospital.

I picked Kevin up at LaGuardia Airport and we went immediately to Flushing Hospital to settle the debt he owed. Unfortunately, the people Kevin needed to see were not working. Kevin was told that he would have to come back. I was upset that it appeared Kevin had not set up an appointment or did not realize that he needed to see specific people in order to reduce the price of his bill.

We left the hospital disappointed but Kevin believed he would be able to solve the problem before he returned to Iowa in a few days. He was excited about being home and wanted to go to his mom's house and see his friends. I dropped him off at CB's house in Merrick and returned to Long Beach. I wished he would have come home with me but accepted the situation as best I could. We made plans for him to come over for lunch the next day. Laura was also disappointed that Kevin didn't return home with me. She had made up welcome signs and put them up both outside and inside our place.

I talked with Rob on the phone for a long time that night about Kevin. We were all so lucky to have such a solid guy like Rob in our lives helping us. We talked for a few hours about possible jobs, careers, and directions for Kevin's future. Rob had taken on the role of a combination of big brother and surrogate father to Kevin and was determined to be successful. I felt like he was a Godsend and I will always be grateful for his enormous efforts.

The next day Kevin called just before he was expected to arrive for lunch to say that he would love to come but his mother was making him rake the leaves at the house in Merrick. Laura and I thought that was strange but we waited for him, nevertheless, to finish that job. We called him several times to find out his estimated time of arrival but he never answered. He called about five hours later and when questioned about the leaves, he said he had been waiting for his uncle Stephen to come over to help. He said Stephen arrived late and after they finished the job, he took a nap. The story sounded like bullshit—like the old drug addict excuses from the past. Later that night, I called CB to ask if she had made Kevin rake the leaves. She said she had asked him but the leaves were still on the ground.

I felt like something had just exploded inside me—a rage that was overpowering. Had Kevin used CB's car to go get high while he was supposed to be with Laura and me? What other reason could there be? The lies were just like old times—detailed, constant lies from a heroin addict. I wanted to call Kevin immediately but I turned first to Holy Spirit as I had been carefully taught to do. My answer from Holy Spirit was clear: ***"Do nothing."***

I sat with that answer for a while but I couldn't accept it. I didn't know if Kevin was doing drugs again. Lying and blowing us off for lunch infuriated me. I turned to Holy Spirit again, and again received the intuition, *"Just let it go."* But the ego had a hold on me. I let the screaming of the ego shout away the quiet advice of my Higher Power. I called Kevin and let him know I knew he was lying about raking the leaves. I told him to go back to Iowa fast before he got in big trouble. I didn't want to hear his lying voice give me denials and excuses. I let him know in no uncertain terms that I wanted nothing more to do with him right now. He continued to call and make excuses and I kept hanging up in a raging fury over his lies. I didn't know if he was using drugs or not. I knew the old familiar lying pattern of the drug addict and that remained with him regardless of whether or not he was using.

Kevin kept calling. He said he wanted to come down to Long Beach and straighten this all out. I said I would meet him on the boardwalk of Long Beach if he came right away. Kevin left his friends and met me at the gazebo on the boardwalk. We got into a shouting match over his lying about why he stood up Laura and me for lunch with the excuse about raking the leaves.

There was nothing he could have said that would have satisfied me. Kevin had lied so many times before and I was so used to him lying his way out of his lies. I continued to shout at him and tell him to go back to Iowa. I couldn't let go of the rage inside me. We parted having great anger at each other.

I was tormented all night long by the rage I had allowed to possess me. The next morning I went over to CB's house in Merrick where Kevin was staying. CB was at work but she had told me she was also suspicious of Kevin. I asked Holy Spirit for help in getting it right this time but when I got to the house I actually woke him up just to get into the same argument again that I had on the boardwalk. After 5 minutes of shouting, I stormed out of the house feeling half crazed. I had gone to the house to talk to him in a kind and loving way and had allowed the old ego thoughts to dominate me again. I sat in my car totally disgusted with myself for not being able to control my ego thought process. This was the lowest I had felt since before Kevin had gone to Iowa.

While I was sitting in the car, overwhelmed by the emotional torment I had put myself through, my cell phone rang and it was Kevin. For 10 minutes I had sat outside the house asking Holy Spirit to help me handle this situation correctly. Now I was given another chance. I told Kevin how miserable I was feeling about this. He said he was feeling the same way and asked me if I would return. I told him that I was still out in front of the house. He came out and got in the car.

I knew I was being given another chance to do a better job of parenting. It was a chance to forgive and to turn over all my rage to Holy Spirit. Kevin said he was sorry for lying. He said he had stopped using drugs but he had not yet stopped his drug addict behavior. He said he fell asleep waiting for his Uncle Stephen to show up to help him. Kevin could understand why I was so upset. Most of the lies in the past were drug related. This one was not. We went out to breakfast at a diner and all the tension and heartache melted away. I was given a chance to forgive him and to forgive myself for my overreaction. We both felt like we learned a lesson.

On the last day of Kevin's visit, he was able to get to Flushing Hospital and his bill was reduced by 90%. On the way to the airport, Kevin said he was glad to be returning to Iowa. He said he felt like Iowa was his home now. Seeing his family and friends was exciting but he felt New York was a dangerous place for him now.

****

Ten days later Laura and I flew out to Iowa for the Thanksgiving holiday. We rented a car and stayed in a hotel close to Rob and Marla's house where Kevin lived. This Thanksgiving was perhaps the best holiday in many years. Kevin was clean and sober and he seemed to have a great attitude toward his recovery. Rob and Marla loved having him in their house as part of the family. He was working as a waiter at the Village Inn and working with Rob on the flood cleanup of the two houses that Rob and his mom own upstate in Iowa.

Kevin also had a girlfriend, Melanie, whom we met out at a local restaurant one night. Melanie is a tall, good looking 24 year old with a lot of personality and self confidence. I liked her right away but was concerned about Kevin being in a relationship so soon after rehab. She also looked like she was too much fun for a guy in the early stages of recovery. But the two of them looked good together and Melanie was well aware of Kevin's status as a recovering heroin addict.

Rob's wife, Marla, and my wife, Laura, hit it off well with each other from the start. Rob and Marla showed us around the Quad Cities straddling the Mississippi River between Iowa and Illinois. Kevin had only been an Iowa resident for about four months but he appeared to fit in fine with everyone there. We went out to restaurants, did a bit of hiking, and had a ridiculously competitive game of monopoly together among Rob, Marla, Kevin, Laura, and me. One would have thought we were all capitalist robber barons by the viciousness with which we played against each other. Nevertheless, we had a lot of laughs and I believe that I must have had a smile on my face for the entire five days I spent in America's heartland.

Without question, the highlight was Thanksgiving dinner at Rob and Marla's house with 34 of their family members and friends. Before dinner, all of us held hands and each person there read a quotation that he/she had picked from a box. Each then described what he or she was thankful for. In addition to their personal gratitude for things in their lives, many of them gave thanks for Kevin, Laura, and me coming to Iowa. They all made us feel so very welcome. There were some tears and many smiles as each person shared feelings. I truly felt that a miracle had taken place as I watched Kevin interact so positively with all of the Iowans. He looked so healthy, so happy. All my prayers had been answered. A few months earlier he was a hopeless drug addict. Now everything looked shiny and new. I was and remain grateful to Rob, Marla, their family and friends, and to my own Higher Power for allowing me to experience such a powerful moment before Thanksgiving dinner. I'm certain that I will retain that memory forever.

****

Back in New York I shared my experience with my Al-Anon family group. Kevin's story had become one of enormous hope for everyone. I was asked to share the story of Kevin at several other Al-Anon meetings in the area and did so enthusiastically. Of course I knew that there was always a chance of relapse. I still wanted to share my strength, hope, and experience with others. My Al-Anon family group had become a valued part of my spiritual life and I reveled in my connection to those involved.

Chapter 32 –
There Are No Accidents

⊱─━━━⊰◆⊱━━━─⊰

Everything seemed to be going well for Kevin in Iowa. He was able to get a part time job as an addiction counselor for gamblers in an organization called Addiction Services of Iowa (A.S.I.). Since he had graduated from NU with a Bachelor of Arts in Social Work, Kevin was certified for the job. He loved it. Kevin didn't have the addiction of gambling but understood the cravings and compulsions of addiction. A.S.I. had done a background check on Kevin that showed no criminal record whatsoever. It is amazing that Kevin managed to live 6 years as an opiate addict—stealing mostly from the people closest to him—forging checks and credit card receipts—pawning his mother's jewelry—and God knows what else that we never found out about—yet remained with a squeaky clean record. He would later admit to his boss about a past addiction to drugs but it was never brought up in an interview.

Now Kevin had two jobs: gambling addiction counselor and waiter at the Village Inn. He also decided to go back to college to attain certification as a radiology / MRI technician. While working at County Community Hospital in New York as a transporter, Kevin had taken an interest in this field and saw it as a possible future. I was overjoyed at the initiative he was taking.

Kevin was now working, going to college, and attending AA meetings. He had a sponsor, a home group, and a completely transformed attitude. He was even receiving outstanding grades in his courses. His job as a gambling addiction counselor would also help him with his own Twelve-Step Program. There is no better way to learn anything well than to actually teach it.

Things were also pretty good with Rob and Marla. Rob complained a bit about Kevin not doing his share of the chores, his slovenliness, and his lateness on bill payments—but was proud of his progress. This was Kevin's first experience in the world as a sober and clean adult. It would take a little time for him to get up to Rob's expectations. Marla and Kevin loved each other and truly enjoyed each other's company. It would be difficult to imagine things going any better than they were.

****

In the middle of March of 2009 Kevin called me, sounding serious, and saying there was something important that he needed to talk to me about. My first inclination was to ask, "Is this a good thing or a bad thing that we're going to talk about?" He said, "Well, it depends how you choose to look at it." I braced myself, not knowing what to expect. Kevin said, "Melanie is pregnant and she is definitely keeping the baby."

I felt like all the blood drained from my head and that I was about to faint with the phone in my hand. I am ashamed to say that my first unspoken thought was, "Is there anything that this kid isn't destined to somehow fuck up?" I'm glad I paused and said nothing because Kevin's next comment totally changed my perception of what was taking place. He said, "You know how you've told me how things that sometimes seem bad at the time often turn out to be the best possible thing that could ever happen? I really think that this is one of those things."

Instantly my entire comportment changed from being disillusioned to surging with tremendous joy that Kevin had actually learned and understood an important metaphysical truth—things are often not as they appear to be. We had talked often about how Kevin's drug addiction, although seeming like a horror in our lives, might actually be the most important experience that Kevin could have ever survived in order to be the man he is capable of becoming.

To hear Kevin use those words in describing an unwanted pregnancy at just the time when he was now recovering from years of addiction . . . well, I was overwhelmed by the apparent wisdom of the statement. Certainly I would not have chosen this time, this place, or this woman to have such an important situation take place in his life. But he was right. How could we know what was needed at this time for the greater good of all concerned?

I thought it would have been better if Kevin and Melanie loved each other. They had considered breaking up just before they found out the news. I would have preferred that he had not engaged in a meaningful romantic relationship in the early months of his recovery. I would have liked him to have established some financial security before taking on fatherhood instead of owing thousands to those who had bailed him out of his drug addiction debt. No, I wouldn't have chosen this at all.

But I know that I can't see what is best in the big picture for all concerned. The birth of a child—my first grandchild—might just be what is best for Kevin, Melanie, and the Universe. Possibly this is just the motivation Kevin needs to grow up fast. There is no way for me to know, so I accept God's plan. There are no accidents. I have faith that everything is meant to happen exactly as it does.

I was pleased that the Holy Spirit allowed me to see this in a positive light. I give great gratitude to my Higher Power for giving me a positive perception of the events. But there was also another voice inside this old football coach's head saying, "Button your chin strap, guys. This game is just beginning."

****

After talking with Rob about Melanie's pregnancy, some fearful thoughts started to form. Rob expressed some misgivings about Kevin's commitment to paying his bills (e.g., car, insurance, phone, cable TV), fulfilling his obligations, and an overall lack of an adult sense of responsibility. I was surprised by Rob's seeming negativity but I listened intently. Rob felt that he was still carrying him and that Kevin was not shouldering his fair share of the burden. That night I called Kevin and confronted him with the revelations I had been given. He immediately flew into a rage. "How could Rob say that? That is so untrue. What is he talking about? He's just like you. Nothing I ever do is good enough for him."

I was stunned by the tirade—particularly the part about nothing he does being good enough for Rob or me. He hung up the phone and decided to confront Rob directly. He was in such a frenzy that Rob felt he had to back him off right away with, "I'm not going to have you talk to me like this in my own house. Calm down or get out." Kevin told me that he couldn't stop crying. He said he hadn't cried like that in a long time.

I'm not sure how the rest of that conversation went except that they ended it on good terms. Kevin told me that Rob denied saying much of what he told me. Rob said that Kevin was so distressed that he did whatever he could just to calm him down. Rob was concerned that neither Kevin nor Melanie was prepared to take on the responsibilities of parenthood.

Rob even offered to adopt the baby if Kevin and Melanie felt overwhelmed by the responsibility. Rob and Marla had lost their only son in his first year of life 18 years ago. Rob's offer was kind and generous but wasn't a consideration for either Kevin or Melanie. Rob would make that offer more than once It was never appreciated as it should have been. From my viewpoint over a thousand miles away, the relationship between Kevin and Rob seemed somewhat damaged. Not a good sign.

Chapter 33 –
Visit to New York

————◆————

Kevin wanted badly to take a trip back to Long Island with Melanie in late May. Working as a gambling addiction counselor, waiting tables, and going to college classes, the end of May would be the only time that he would have the chance to come home with his pregnant girlfriend. It also coincided with the NCAA lacrosse championships during Memorial Day weekend when I was having people over to watch the games. The timing seemed good for a visit and both Kevin and Melanie could fly "stand-by" for free with his Uncle Larry's airlines privileges.

I picked up Kevin and Melanie at LaGuardia airport and brought them back to Long Beach. I took a long walk on the boardwalk and along the beach with both of them. Melanie had never seen the ocean before and I was thrilled to be walking with them, talking about Kevin's recovery and the battles that we've had in the past trying to get him clean. Kevin talked openly about his exploits as a drug addict and we also talked about the possibility of my writing a book regarding our experience with his drug addiction.

I asked Melanie if finding out about Kevin's past with the lying, stealing, and violence caused her any shock or doubts about the kind of man who was now her partner. Melanie said that Kevin had told her a lot about it and that she might even know things that I didn't. She said since she has known Kevin, she has seen no sign of that guy whom we were discussing. That sounded great to me. Melanie just seemed so unspoiled and down to earth. I liked her the first time I met her over Thanksgiving and I liked her even more at this moment.

I dropped off Kevin and Melanie at CB's house after lunch and we made plans for them to come over that night for pizza. Matt and Jillian were also coming over. Kevin was in a great mood when he arrived but he was so tired that he really looked stoned. He even kind of acted stoned—being touchy—feely with everyone. I told him that he looked high and he laughed saying that he hadn't slept at all last night. I found it impossible to believe that he could have gone and gotten drugs as soon as he arrived in New York but he did have the opportunity. Melanie said he left the house to see one of his friends shortly after I dropped them off. Everyone was so happy that night that I didn't want to think it was even possible.

The next day Kevin stopped by my Sherwood lacrosse practice and he gave me some bad news. He said that he and Melanie had been fighting non-stop. He said that they definitely do not love each other and seem to be totally incompatible. He said she doesn't want to do anything or go anywhere with him, so he's just leaving her in Merrick with his mom or alone and going out to see people on his own. According to Kevin, Melanie was a psycho bitch who just wanted to make him miserable. This was sad news.

Still, Kevin seemed to want to do right by Melanie concerning the baby. It just appeared to me that he had a lot of heartache ahead of him if Melanie was as nasty as he portrayed. I was surprised that I misread her because I certainly liked what I saw. Nevertheless, Kevin painted a picture of her as an unstable woman who was determined to make him unhappy.

Saturday was the "Final Four" party at our house for the NCAA Division 1 lacrosse semifinals. My two sons, their girlfriends, my nephew Stephen, and members of my lacrosse coaching staff were all in attendance. The games were both blowouts but everyone had a great time. Kevin and Melanie seemed okay but they certainly didn't show any affection to each other.

I was also concerned that I couldn't get a good grip on Kevin's recovery program. He had not attended any meetings since coming to New York. He went from party to party among his friends and family, albeit without drinking. He never spoke of the Twelve Step program or his sponsor. I certainly was not looking for trouble and felt that if he was not drinking or drugging, I could not complain. I certainly would have felt more secure if I had seen some sign of dedication to his program. When asked, he did speak about his job helping gambling addicts and I wondered if that was all he needed of a program to stay clean and sober.

I didn't see Kevin on Sunday but on Monday he came over with my brother Mike and my nephew Stephen for the championship game between Syracuse and Cornell. Kevin did not bring Melanie, however. It was great to see Kevin together with his uncle and cousin. The game was one of the most incredible in all of lacrosse history with Syracuse scoring in the final few seconds to tie the game and then winning in overtime. I had wished Melanie was there because she had no feelings for lacrosse and that game would have made a convert of any sports fan.

I took Kevin aside and asked why Melanie didn't come with him. He said that she was just doing anything she could to sabotage his fun on his return home. I hated hearing that. If it were true, there would be many tough moments ahead for the two of them. Having a baby together is not a good situation for a couple who are at each other's throat. All I could do was hand it over to my Higher Power and hope for the best.

I wanted to see Melanie one more time before I took them to the airport for the return to Iowa. I offered to take the two of them out for lunch at Rachel's Cafe on Woodcleft canal in Freeport and they accepted. I invited my buddy, Doc, to join us. Doc was the rival coach at Forest City when Kevin was a Sherwood player and they had established a good relationship over the years. Doc and I were buddies and often ate lunch together. We had talked about Kevin's situation and at age 68, Doc was still a charmer with the young ladies. I knew Melanie would enjoy his company.

Lunch was fun for everyone except me. I couldn't help but think that Kevin looked drugged. He seemed euphoric and his eyes seemed glazed. "Could he really be high?" I wondered. I certainly did not want to ruin everyone's time by bringing it up, but I was disturbed.

His lips and tongue were all white and he just looked and acted high. Doc never mentioned anything and was busy charming Melanie with his Irish wit and personality.

While we were waiting for our food Kevin saw his old middle school wrestling coach, Nick Dondero, and eagerly went over to say hello. Doc went to the bathroom, so I had Melanie alone and asked her, "What's up with Kevin?"

Melanie said, "He just seems like he's a bit off somehow today." I was glad she noticed it too but she made no further comment and we let it go at that. Kevin and Doc both returned to the table and we had a nice lunch while watching the fishing boats come in and out of the canal. I was uncomfortable for the rest of the meal and wondered if I was making something out of nothing.

We all said goodbye to Doc and I drove Kevin and Melanie back to Merrick. They were leaving for the airport at 4am. Since I was their driver, we decided that they should sleep over my place so we could leave straight for the airport from Long Beach.

I told Laura about how I perceived Kevin's demeanor and appearance to be at lunch and she said that something seemed wrong. After commiserating over what to do about it, we decided that nothing good could come from making the accusation. If he was back on drugs it would certainly show itself sooner or later and neither of us was absolutely sure.

I picked them up in Merrick that night and brought them back to Long Beach. When Laura got me alone she said, "Something is definitely not right with him." Matt lived down the street so he came over to spend time with us. Since Matt didn't bring up anything about Kevin, I just left it alone. At 3:30am we left for LaGuardia and I kissed and hugged them both goodbye.

I was left wondering if I was imagining it. If he was using drugs in New York, would he stop because he had no connection in Iowa? Was there anything that I should be doing that I wasn't? I was glad that I could hand it over to the Holy Spirit and let Him decide for me.

****

When I got home from the airport I decided to do a contemplation.

Question: How do I handle my suspicions that Kevin was not straight or clean when he was here in New York?

My thoughts: Kevin looked high to me several times during the last week but particularly while having lunch with Doc. His eyes looked glazed and he seemed to slur his words and act high. Accusing him would have caused a lot of problems, and I don't know how to pursue my suspicions. It seems like it is out of my hands, but I'd sure like to know.

> **Pray for Grace, followed by meditation.**
> *Answer: No matter what my suspicions, Kevin has to go through his own karma and I'm not supposed to investigate. If it's a problem, it will surface sooner or later. Love Kevin anyway—don't press the issue at all. Continue to encourage him to pick up the pace of his recovery. Write a letter to that effect if it makes you feel comfortable. Don't tell him of your suspicions—he might already know. Stay with unconditional love— non-judgment—total forgiveness. This is a solid answer to your question. Choose if you would follow it.*

Chapter 34 –
Writing a Book

Although we suspected Kevin of relapsing in New York, we weren't 100% sure. In most ways it seemed too bizarre to imagine him being clean for 9 months and then bringing his pregnant girlfriend home to New York in order to start using again. Although my imagination had the tendency to run wild with the possibilities of what was going on with him, my Inner Guidance was directing me to **"let go and let God."** If Kevin had relapsed, there was no way it wouldn't show up sooner or later.

I didn't talk about my suspicions to anyone except Laura. At my Al-Anon meetings I had become a voice of experience, strength, and hope for the group. I had often spoken of the possibilities of relapse and how my faith in the Twelve Step program did not depend on whether or not Kevin relapsed. I felt a strong attachment to my Al-Anon family groups in Long Beach that I connected with on Saturdays and Sundays. Sharing at "step meetings" and listening to others felt like a spiritual connection. I felt all of them to be like spiritual brothers and sisters to me. I could easily accept any defects in character that any of them had. I felt love, non-judgment, and compassion at the meetings. I felt like I was part of the solution instead of part of the problem.

My desire to write a book on the experience of being the father of a drug addict seemed to be getting stronger but I wanted to be certain that it wasn't my ego that was driving this.

Larry Glenz

****

Question: *Am I destined to write and publish a book that is inspired by my connection to Holy Spirit?*

My thoughts: *I have the ability to tell a story but it's usually been verbal instead of on paper. I have a desire to serve Spirit in whatever way that I am directed. I seem to have been brought to the problem of drug addiction, and writing a book could be a way to help others. The book will have to include spiritual ideas from A Course in Miracles, Alcoholics Anonymous, and Al-Anon. Once I have a book, speaking engagements could more easily follow. I would love to help others who have the same or a similar problem.*

I want to make sure that I am guided by Holy Spirit in this. Certainly I wish it to be written by Him and scribed through me. I know this is how it should come to me.

> **Pray for grace, followed by meditation:**
> **Answer: "Of course you should write a book; and it will come through Spirit as long as you turn to Spirit as you write it. I will guide you over the rocks and pitfalls, as long as you stay with Spirit. Yes, it will be a lot about turning to Jesus or Holy Spirit. You will honest about your own failings—you will portray CB accurately as a loving mother with an enabling personality. You will also include her input into the story. That will have a healing effect on your relationship and your family as a whole. The book will take at least 2 years. The story isn't over. Kevin's challenges continue although they may or may not be drug related. Teaching people to turn to Spirit is your function. This book will bring you closer to God because you will be required to connect with Holy Spirit each time you write. Enjoy the process; it's a labor of love."**

Over the next week I became concerned that I might be coming from the ego mind instead of my connection to my Higher Power

156

when writing the book. I was still afraid what others would think of my motivation, but I was mostly afraid that my ego would trick me into thinking that I was receiving Inner Guidance when it was the ego's motivation. I figured I better check in with my Higher Power for clarification.

Question: *How can I be sure it is You, Holy Spirit Who guides my writing for this book?*

My thoughts: *Sometimes I feel that this book is just something to calm my ego because in retirement I'm not doing anything impressive in the eyes of others. I want to stop now if it is not Your Will and in the greater interest of all. I want to be reassured that this is Your project, Holy Spirit, and that I am Your scribe.*

I am concerned that Kevin, CB, and others may see this as something to make myself look good at their expense. I ask You to give me confidence that this is not the case. My intention here is to gain reassurance from You that You are guiding my efforts.

> **Pray for Grace—followed by meditation:**
> **Answer: "I have called to you, My Son, and you have answered Me. I called to you a long time before you chose to listen. ACIM was the vehicle you chose to reach Me. Your divorce was the pain that motivated you to look for "a better way."**
> **Since you started your awakening process in 1994, you have increasingly turned to Me and your peace and joy have increased accordingly. This past year you have moved quickly in your spiritual practice and have placed yourself in a position to heal your brothers, who are My sons.**
> **Like Kevin's addiction has brought you closer to Me, this book will do the same. Rest assured this is My project for the healing of your brothers. Don't worry how it will all come together. You have My promise that, as long as you turn to Me, I will guide you in every step. You**

> *have an important story; don't worry about making it interesting with your own clever personality. Leave that to Me. Remember it will take some time—more than a year—particularly to get it published and out to the brothers who need it. Be patient. Write when I nudge you. Put no pressure on yourself. Enjoy the process. Tell anyone you want about it. Thank you for your efforts."*

****

Kevin's addiction and the writing of this book are strengthening my connection to my Higher Power. I feel that my function is to help others to do the same. All I need to do is open my mind to the awareness of God's presence and guidance to let this happen.

Chapter 35 –
Kevin's Confession

A few days later I received a prompt to write a handwritten letter to Kevin about forgiveness. He mentioned earlier in the week that there were things he did as a drug addict that he had never shared with me. He said it was bad and that he was ashamed. We didn't take it any further on the phone but it stayed in my mind that there were things he might feel are unforgiveable. I let Holy Spirit take the lead in writing the letter about forgiveness and I have no conscious memory of what I wrote.

The following week Kevin told me the story of how, in the months before he left for Iowa, he was part of a three man team that would shoot people with a taser gun at ATMs and steal their money. He certainly was not the brains of the outfit, but he was the actual assailant. One guy served as the lookout for easy marks, another was the get-away driver. Kevin was the one who actually shot the people with the taser and stole the money. He got anywhere from $20-$300. He wore a mask. He said the person would be stunned for about 10 seconds. Kevin would then take the wallet—grab the money—throw the wallet on the ground—and run to the get-away car. They immediately went to the drug dealer to score heroin with the stolen money.

Kevin admitted he was ashamed of this but also said that he got a "rush" out of it at the time because he knew he was going to get high. He also said his mom's car was sometimes used to get away. One of his partners in crime had since been arrested for a different armed robbery crime and supposedly is looking at a long prison sentence.

I asked Kevin how he turned out to be the mugger instead of the lookout or get-away driver. He said that he was easily the fastest and strongest of the three. He also had no police record nor had he been fingerprinted like the others had. The other two were more experienced in setting up the crime—picking who to hit, where and when to do it, and they provided the taser gun. He said they were desperate from being dope sick and this seemed the fastest way to get money. He knew it was wrong, but getting high quickly was imperative.

It was now making sense why Kevin had accepted Rob and Marla's offer to go to Iowa. He was scared. He was in too deep. He was badly addicted, no job, no money, and had become a serious criminal. He must have realized that prison was in his near future and a life in Iowa supported by loved ones was an escape.

His girlfriend told me that he admitted to her that he had four bags of heroin taped to his leg when he got on the plane for Iowa. He said that he didn't expect to get into a rehab immediately upon arriving. When he found out that he was going to be admitted the next day, he shot up the stash he had brought with him before entering the facility, rather than waste it.

Listening to Kevin tell me the story over the phone wasn't easy. He deserved to be in prison. Nevertheless, he had been spared that consequence, and I hoped and believed that he would be able to help others in the world as a recovering addict. There must be a reason why all this has all unfolded as it has. There is no way for me to know this so I must trust in my Higher Power and let Him handle the details.

Chapter 36 –
Relapse and Deception

⟟n early September of 2009 I received a call from Rob. I knew CB had gone out to Iowa for Melanie's baby shower. Rob indicated that there were some bad signs coming from Kevin. Rob suspected a relapse. He said Kevin had been taking out Pay Day Loans at 455% APR and that he was receiving calls all day long from them asking to speak to Kevin about payment. Rob further explained that Kevin wasn't paying his bills and had been asking to borrow more money to make his car payment that was in Rob's name. Rob had also inadvertently seen Kevin in a bad part of town where he would be able to score drugs. He didn't have any real proof but his suspicions were strong. Of course, Kevin denied there was a problem.

Laura had called Melanie about an undelivered baby shower gift that we had sent her. As the conversation evolved, Melanie related to her that she believed that Kevin had relapsed. Despite making a good salary, Kevin was getting deeper in debt with the Pay Day Loans. She believed there was no other explanation for the absence of money because Melanie said that they rarely go anywhere or buy anything other than necessities.

When CB returned from Iowa I told her of my suspicions and that both Rob and Melanie said that something was wrong. She said that it was possible. However, she didn't see any evidence of it while she was staying there with them.

I received a call from Kevin the next day. He was upset that I had told his mother that I suspected he had relapsed. He said, "Why

161

didn't you ever say anything to me if you suspected me of using drugs?" I explained to him that I wasn't looking for trouble and believed that if it were true, it would surface soon enough.

Kevin assured me that the greatest thing he had ever accomplished was to get off of heroin. He said one of the great parts of kicking the drug habit was the restoration of the great relationship with his father. He went on further to say that if he ever was going to relapse, the fact that he was to become a father in a few weeks would most certainly end that possibility.

He was speaking with pride and passion about the value of his sobriety. I told him that I believed him, saying "You've made my day." When I returned home I told Laura that there was no way Kevin was back on drugs. If he were, he should be an Oscar award winning actor. He was that convincing.

I was thinking that if he was lying to me with this much conviction and passion, it would be difficult to ever believe anything he said to me again. But after talking with Melanie a few days later, I found out that Kevin was indeed lying. She admitted that Kevin had relapsed four months earlier when he was in New York. Ever since then she and Kevin's relationship changed. She said she couldn't trust him anymore. She had watched him lie to everyone while he was in New York—accepting all their praise for staying clean while he was getting high every day.

It was Kevin's relapse in New York that caused the problems between the two of them. For the past four months we were listening to Kevin's description of Melanie as an unstable, psycho bitch. Melanie never told me of his relapse because Kevin had begged her not to, promising that it was just a brief flirtation with the drug before the baby arrived. She would need to depend on his salary after the baby arrived and felt trapped. She caught him in a series of lies at the same time that his money was disappearing and he was going into debt with the Pay Day Loans. Although she had no definitive proof that he was back on the opiates—heroin or Oxycontin—she knew. Still Kevin vehemently denied it all.

Melanie had felt all alone for four months keeping Kevin's secret. Now she realized that was a big mistake. Just a month before the baby was due, Kevin was addicted and in debt. His job as gambling addiction counselor provided the money she would be depending upon to sustain them. Kevin was a fraud as an addiction counselor. He was an active intravenous heroin user giving advice to others about addiction.

My contemplations with Holy Spirit continued to advise me to use patience, compassion, and unconditional love with Kevin. Nevertheless, when I was awakened in the middle of the night by a phone call from Melanie, I was ready to spring into action once again as the responsible father who needed to fix Kevin before the baby was born.

Melanie had checked Kevin's car after he had fallen asleep to see if she could get some concrete evidence of Kevin's relapse. In the trunk of his car was a duffle bag with needles, syringes, spoons, and other drug paraphernalia. She also found text messages on his cell phone referring to Oxycontin. With this evidence, Kevin could no longer deny his relapse.

****

After getting off the phone I turned to my Inner Guidance.

Question: Do I go to Iowa and try to get Kevin back into rehab?

My Thoughts: Now that there is no doubt about Kevin's relapse, I'm stuck with the thought, "What do I do about it?" Throwing him into rehab hasn't worked, but it stands a better chance than continuing to use. My thoughts right now are to fly to Iowa, stay with Rob, and come up with a plan with Kevin as what to do. There are no easy answers, so I'm planning on following Spirit's advice as I receive it.

> **Pray for Grace, followed by meditation:**
> **Answer: Yes, go out there. Be a reassuring father and tell him that he can clean up before the baby comes. Your presence there has the best chance of success. There is no other course of action other than detox—rehab—recovery. Convince him to try again. The baby is a**

> **motivating force for Kevin. Let's use it now. Laura will support you.**

****

I stayed up all night making flight plans to get to Iowa quickly. When Laura awoke, she did indeed encourage me to go out there immediately. She helped me to book a flight for the following morning. I called Rob to tell him of the revelations and asked if I could stay at his house for four days while I worked on getting Kevin back into the Country Forest rehab. I made plans to rent a car. We fully expected that Kevin would resist going back to inpatient rehab at Country Forest because it would certainly jeopardize his job. I had made up my mind that the job didn't matter. What good is an addiction counselor who is actively shooting dope into his arm?

When Kevin found out from Melanie that I knew, he called me several times. I didn't pick up but I texted him, "Just give me a day to sit with this. I promise to talk tomorrow. Not today please." I didn't want him to know I was flying in and I didn't want to have to lie about it. He texted back, "It's not as bad as you think."

This was a familiar pattern. Kevin denies using drugs until there is ironclad evidence against him. When he's busted, he minimizes the amount he uses. He will say that he was curious and experimented with it a bit—but that it was all over. He would refuse to go back to Country Forest saying that I was overreacting to the problem. I had been through all this before. I knew that, as much as I hated it, there was more for me to learn. This was my classroom.

Chapter 37 –
Five Days in Iowa

I was a volunteer assistant coach for the Sherwood JV football team, so I needed an excuse to tell the team and coaches why I would be missing the Lawrence game. Rather than bring up Kevin's situation, I said there was a death in the family and no further questions were asked. Laura dropped me off at LaGuardia Airport at about 5AM. I would have plenty of time alone to figure things out with the help of my Higher Power.

One thing about my approach to this was bothering me. For years now I had received the same message from my Inner Guidance to let go of trying to fix Kevin. Now here I was flying to the Midwest to fix Kevin by forcing him back into rehab. He would never acquiesce to inpatient rehab without force. We had leverage to use against him. Rob owns his car. Melanie could kick him out of their apartment by threatening to expose his drug use to authorities—leaving him homeless. We could go to his boss and expose his drug use. After all, he had needle tracks on his arms.

We had leverage to force him back into rehab, but the use of force has consistently been discouraged by Holy Spirit over these years of contemplations. This was confusing me. Something just didn't feel right.

Certainly I could justify using all the leverage at my disposal because of the urgency of getting Kevin clean before the birth of their baby. I also knew Kevin was going to go crazy over this. I knew the pattern that this would take. Kevin would deny everything that could not be completely proven and greatly minimize anything that could be. For example, I could expect Kevin to say that the syringes in the bag were from months ago and that he was no longer using. He would steadfastly refuse to go back to Country Forest but would consent to an outpatient program of his own choosing.

Outpatient treatment after a relapse has always been his way of pacifying the pressure being put on him to get back into recovery, but he never took it seriously. I called it "Recovery Lite." It was his way to get me off his back and still continue using. I felt that I couldn't let him get away with that trick again. Yet I still didn't feel right about forcing him against his will. If I had learned anything, it was that recovery has to come from within the addict. All rehab efforts pushed upon him by me had ultimately failed, although the Country Forest experience lasted three times longer than the rest. *A Course in Miracles* clearly teaches that nothing good can come from using guilt to get others to behave.

****

I arrived in Moline Airport on the Illinois side of the Quad Cities. I rented a small Toyota and crossed the Mississippi into Davenport, Iowa. I gave Melanie a call knowing that she had to go to work as a waitress at Ruby Tuesdays within the hour. Knowing that Melanie had no car and usually took a bus to work, I asked if I could give her a ride. She gave me directions and I had no problem finding their apartment.

Although Melanie was 8 months pregnant, she still looked long, lean and beautiful. It just looked like she was hiding a volleyball up front under her clothes. We talked a short while about Kevin and how things had changed between them since they went to New York. She expressed how alone she had felt carrying Kevin's secret with no one to tell. It was apparent that she understood what a mistake it was to guard his secret. I drove Melanie to work at the restaurant and we made plans to get Kevin over to Rob's house that night without his knowing I was in town. We had to start the process of getting him back into recovery.

Rob was at work when I arrived at his house and Marla was away for two days on a golf outing with a group of her friends—"the Dames" they called themselves. Rob had left the key in the mailbox and I made myself comfortable in their home. To my surprise, there was a six month old puppy in the kitchen. I spent the day playing with "Samson" and walking him around Davenport on his retractable leash—all the while asking my Higher Power to help me make the right moves with Kevin.

Rob arrived home in the early evening. It was obvious that Kevin's relapse had taken a toll on him. He was both sad and angry at his perceived failure. He and Marla both felt that they had failed and wondered what they could have done differently. It amazed me that Rob could possibly feel any guilt after all that he had done for Kevin. That seems to be the effect this disease has upon the family.

Rob gave me some of Kevin's mail that he had not picked up. Rob said they were bills, speeding tickets, and Pay Day Loans that had not been paid. Since I wouldn't get the truth from Kevin, I decided to open them. It quickly became obvious that Kevin had gotten himself in debt and was taking out Pay Day Loans at exorbitant interest rates.

Since Rob and Kevin had been at odds with each other in recent weeks, I asked him how we were going to get Kevin to come to his house so we could start to face this issue of relapse. Rob said that if Kevin were told that he had ordered pizza, he'd be there. Rob called Melanie and invited the two of them over while we went out to get the pizza. I was wondering how Kevin would react to my surprise visit.

As we pulled up to Rob's house with the pizza, we saw Kevin and Melanie arriving. I couldn't get over Kevin's appearance. He was rail thin, pale, unshaven, and unkempt. When he saw me get out of the car, he gave me a smile with a sort of disbelieving shake of his head. I was stunned when I saw from his smile that he was missing one of his front teeth. Was this really my handsome son of just a few months ago? He looked like a poster boy for heroin addiction. He said with a shake of the head, "I should have figured it wouldn't take long for you to get out here to Iowa."

From past experience I knew the first night was going to be filled with anger and hysterics on Kevin's part. It was now Friday night. I expected a full blown battle from him for the entire weekend. I hoped by Sunday night when the Giants played the Cowboys on national TV that Kevin would have settled into the idea of going back to rehab and getting a fresh start in anticipation of the baby's arrival. I still couldn't believe we were going to have to go through all this again! My flight home was scheduled for Tuesday. I had given myself an extra day if he refused to go into treatment on Monday. I was still uncomfortable with my plan to use force or leverage to get him to acquiesce if he continued resistance.

The first night went pretty much as I expected. Rob, Melanie, Kevin, and I all sat around the dining room table. After a little bit of small talk, I asked Kevin to tell me what had happened. As expected, he minimized the extent of his drug use and the amount of the financial debt he had recently accumulated. When I recited some of his unpaid bills and loans from the mail I had opened, he flew into an indignant rage over my violating his privacy. I reminded him that he owed me thousands and, despite his promises, had paid me virtually nothing. I also repeated a litany of lies he had recently told me and I expressed no remorse over opening bills to get to the truth.

It soon became obvious that there was going to be no civil or rational conversation between us, so I figured I'd get right to the point. "Kevin, I am out here for one reason, to get you back into Country Forest and recommitted to recovery before your baby is born." Defiantly he replied, "Well, that's not going to happen." The battle had begun.

Melanie, Rob, and I were all united in our purpose but I was the only one who had experienced what was about to take place. Kevin reacted like a caged animal, yet his rage and indignation seemed to scare no one. We all felt that we couldn't back down to this active junkie and the chaos he was causing. With the impending arrival of his baby, there was too much at stake now to let this continue.

After a series of angry exchanges, Rob asked Kevin to come outside to get him away from me for a while. Rob was going to try the "good cop" routine to calm him down. I knew that it would be days before there was any chance of Kevin seeing rehab as being his best option. I looked at Melanie to see her reaction. It was clear to me that she was glad that the process had started. She had felt so alone in all this over the past four months.

Rob had returned without Kevin after what sounded like a shouting match. Kevin had turned over the duffle bag from his car trunk to Rob and walked home. Rob dropped the bag on the dining room table and unzipped it. Indeed, there must have been two dozen syringes, cigarette lighters, a big metal spoon with the remnants of burned heroin or Oxycontin all over it, and an exercise hand grip used by Kevin to pump up his veins before injecting himself. The sight of the drug paraphernalia coincided with the nauseous feeling in the pit of my stomach.

Rob then took me outside to see Kevin's car. The arm rest on the driver's side of Kevin's car had multiple burn marks from where he cooked the opiates in the big spoon with the lighter before bringing it into the syringe. The car was a mess with Taco Bell, McDonald's and other fast food wrappers all over the floor and the back seats. In the glove compartment were the receipts of the Pay Day Loans Kevin had taken and the canceled checks for those that he had paid back.

The evidence of the obvious drug abuse and the financial debt—combined with his hideous, emaciated appearance, highlighted by the missing front tooth—all led me to believe things were worse than I had even imagined. Kevin, as I expected, was determined to avoid inpatient rehab and keep his job as a gambling addiction counselor. Despite the evidence, he was maintaining his story of only limited drug use and insisted that it was weeks ago. He also saw no conflict with the fact that he refused to go back into recovery for himself but still believed he was an effective addiction counselor for others.

Kevin had been gone about 20 minutes when my cell phone rang. In a calm, peaceful, unthreatening voice, Kevin asked, "What day is your flight home, Dad?" His survival instincts had kicked in. He just had to avoid going to Country Forest until I was gone. I didn't answer him and decided not to let him know I had only five days before my return flight to New York.

I offered Kevin the opportunity to prove that he was clean by taking a drug test. Naturally, he refused. I offered him $100 if he was clean. He said, "I don't want your money." I offered $200. Again he refused. I said, "I hear you've been selling your blood plasma for cash, Kevin. This is easy money if you're clean, like you insist. I'll pick you up in the morning with Rob to go to Country Forest." He hung up.

The next morning Rob and I were at Kevin and Melanie's apartment to take him for a drug test. Although we were successful in getting him in the car, the conversation quickly became harsh. Before long, Kevin had bolted out the back door of the car and decided to walk home from wherever we were in Davenport. He then took his car from Rob's house with his spare key and hid it.

Rob and I decided to go to Country Forest to see what our options were. We looked for the boss, Darryl Johnson, with whom Rob had conversed two days earlier. We found Darryl outside on the grounds of the rehab riding a John Deere tractor. This scene was quite different from the rehabs in New York, for sure. Darryl recognized Rob and turned off the tractor. After exchanging a few pleasantries, Rob explained that I had come from NY to get Kevin back into rehab. I asked him if he had any advice for me and he did.

Darryl had been a heroin addict until the age of 31. He was now my age, 59. He said, "Look, I loved the stuff and I would have continued to use and would use now if there were no consequences. But there are big consequences. He's not going to stop unless the pain outweighs the gain. Therefore, you are right to use everything at your disposal to get him into recovery. Take away the car, tell his boss, have Melanie throw him out and threaten to deny him rights to see the baby—anything. Make him see the consequences of drug addiction."

Darryl warned, "I can't tell you how many family members have told me they would just pray and leave it to God. Then when the guy was in the coffin, they deeply regretted not doing all that was in their physical power to stop him. If you do all you can and your son dies—you won't have any of those regrets. You'll know you did all you could. And, if he dies, it was God's plan that he pass on. That's my advice and my experience."

Before thanking Darryl, I silently thanked my Higher Power for sending that advice to me and asked Him to continue to guide me. Still, this advice sounded more like what the original drug counselors had given me from the Pemto recovery program on Long Island years earlier. It was not what I had come to learn from Al-Anon, to let go and let God.

Darryl suggested we do a "civil committal" on Kevin. If two people file a complaint with the court claiming that Kevin is creating an unsafe environment for Melanie and her unborn baby, a judge can order the police to pick up Kevin at home or at his job and take him to Country Forest. There will be a hearing with a judge who can order Kevin into a mandatory inpatient recovery program.

That solution seemed extreme to me, but I was glad to have the option. It could be used as a last resort if he refused to go into a recovery program by Monday. My plan, however, was to wear him down over the next few days so that he would see a voluntary return to Country Forest as his best option. I had been successful with this approach in the past and believed I could pull it off.

The Giants were playing the Cowboys in an NFL game on Sunday night. We are both big Giant fans. My plan was to get Kevin to give in to treatment by the end of the game and commit to go into the Country Forest facility on Monday morning. I had two days to wear him down. I still couldn't believe I was doing this again.

****

On Saturday night I asked Melanie if she would like to go out to dinner somewhere of her choosing. She accepted gratefully. Kevin apparently never took her out anywhere—saving whatever money he had for drugs. When I arrived to pick her up, I heard violent screaming coming from the apartment complex. I ran up the stairs to see Kevin restraining Melanie from behind her with a wrestling hold while she screamed and fought to get loose. Kevin's face was cut. He was bleeding and he was furious. He let go of Melanie as I was running up the stairs and she immediately ran downstairs to get away.

I said, "What the hell are you doing Kevin—beating up your girlfriend? He screamed, "Me? Look at my face. That bitch ripped my shirt, scratched up my face, and broke my eye glasses. I can't see without those glasses." I decided not to push it at that stage because nothing good was going to come out of it if I stayed there. Melanie was safe in my car and I decided to leave before things got worse. Kevin ran down the stairs to scream at Melanie to ask her where his backup eyeglasses were. The car doors were locked and he was banging on the car with a look of violent lunacy. He punched the car as I pulled away. I watched him in his raging fury through my rearview mirror.

I looked at Melanie to see if she was alright. She had a little nick on her finger from where she scratched Kevin. She was completely calm. Surprising, when you consider she had just been in a choke hold a minute earlier. I asked if she was okay. She said quietly, "Yeah, I think so." I asked what happened.

She said she had been downstairs waiting for me to arrive. She was trying to stay away from Kevin who had been harassing her in the apartment about going out to dinner and playing the role of "nice girl" with his father. He came downstairs and menacingly said, "Come on, don't you want to give me a big hug?" As she pushed him away, Kevin grabbed her purse. Any money she had in the world was in that purse, as you can't leave money around when your boyfriend is a heroin addict. In her desperate effort to get it back, she ripped his shirt halfway off, scratched his face, and took his glasses which she purposely broke and threw away. When I came up the stairs, Kevin was actually defending himself from a wildcat. I had to laugh. Kevin had started the trouble, but this girl could really handle herself.

Melanie picked out a nice restaurant in downtown Davenport and I had a fascinating time getting to know this beautiful 25 year old woman who was carrying my first grandchild. She was so down to earth and so emotionally strong in handling the difficult situation of being eight months pregnant with the baby of a father that had recently relapsed on heroin.

Melanie had plans to go into the army before she found herself to be with child. She had little money, little education, and believed she would be serving tables her whole life if she didn't do something herself to change that. Although I never pictured a soldier looking quite as good as Melanie, I am certain that she would have been a good one. But now that plan was off the table, at least for the time being.

We got to know a lot more about each other during dinner. I think Melanie could tell that I really liked her and planned on being supportive of her situation as it existed. I'm sure she could also tell how much I loved Kevin despite his behavior as a drug addict for the past seven years. We felt that we had an ally in each other, both in wanting to do what was best for Kevin and best for the unborn baby who was due in less than a month.

When we finished dinner, Melanie met up with her friend, Jennifer, and went to her house to watch a movie. I wanted to see Kevin and try to talk some sense into him about returning to rehab. He angrily told me he wanted nothing to do with me. In fact, he said, "All you want to do is destroy my life." And I knew at that moment that he actually believed it. Drug addiction is a disease of the mind.

I went over to his apartment even though he told me not to come. I wanted to tell him that night that if he didn't volunteer to go back to Country Forest on Monday, that I would go to his boss and tell him of his relapse into heroin addiction. I told Kevin exactly that when I arrived, and as I expected, he totally flipped out. Nevertheless, I wanted that seed planted in his head that night so that he would tire of resisting by Sunday night. He needed some time to come to the conclusion that a return to Country Forest was his best option. He could be clean by the birth of the baby and ready to take care of his family.

His rage scared me a little and I felt I better get out of there before it became a physical fight. He followed me out to my car cursing me out the entire way. As I held my ground, Kevin's face became almost demonic. He said, "That's it, I'm going to kill myself," and ran back into his apartment.

I paused for a few minutes to consider my next move. Since he was strung out on heroin and emotionally insane, I thought that I might not want to take that threat too lightly. I went back into his apartment but I could tell if I stayed, he was ready to physically attack me. Realizing that Kevin was dangerous, I decided to leave and think the situation over.

Rob's house was empty. Rob had gone to spend the night with his brother and Marla was still away on her golf outing with her girlfriends. I had plenty of time to be with myself and contemplate what I was doing with the advice of my Divine Inspiration. I turned to Him for help. As I sat in meditation, my cell phone rang. It was Kevin. He shouted, "Go home and stay the fuck out of my life. You hear me?"

I told him I couldn't do that. "There is too much at stake here, Kevin. You're going to be a father in a few weeks. Melanie and the baby need you to be clean." He said, "I'm going to kill myself but I'm not going down alone, you understand!" The phone went dead.

Although I believed that Kevin was not capable of that level of violence against himself or others, I called Melanie and asked her if she could stay at her friend's house for the night. She agreed after I told her of the conversation. But once again, I detected no fear or panic in her voice. She was concerned but steady as a rock. I couldn't help but think, "This girl has courage."

****

I decided to do a contemplation to get further confirmation that I was doing the right thing.

Contemplation on 9/20/09

Question: Am I getting the right message from You, Holy Spirit, to force Kevin back into rehab?

My thoughts: Kevin's violence and rage at me threatening to tell his boss about his addiction certainly hasn't brought me peace. If I am to "choose peace first," it doesn't seem like that is what I am doing. The message from Spirit has been, "Let go and let God." I've been advised, "I need do nothing." I could do that instead, but it leaves the problem to linger instead of getting him clean and ready for a new try at recovery. I asked for help yesterday and believed Darryl's advice at Country Forest—to use everything at my disposal—was Spirit's answer to me. Now I have doubts again. I'm asking for clear advice.

> **Pray for Grace, followed by meditation:**
> **Answer:** *"Choosing peace first means to choose the situation that will ultimately bring peace. Have no more doubts. You have let this play out—and now it is a no brainer. He has threatened to kill himself, take someone else down with him, and has committed an act of violence against Melanie as recently as yesterday. He's desperate—but be gentle, loving, and firm."*

****

The next morning, Sunday, Rob and I went over to Kevin's apartment to talk to Kevin again. Kevin remembered little of the dramatic threats that he made the night before and denied that he ever intended violence against anyone.

Rob did most of the talking. Kevin was stretched out on his couch while Rob was sitting in a chair with his face just inches away from Kevin's. Rob was giving an old school pep talk, giving Kevin lots of advice and reminding him of his responsibilities to Melanie and the unborn baby. I was surprised that Kevin calmly agreed to everything Rob was saying, without adding any dialogue of his own.

Rob passionately reminded Kevin that he and Marla's own child, Nicholas, had died in his first year of life without ever having the chances that Kevin has had in the world. He couldn't understand how Kevin could consider wasting his life on drugs when he had been presented with such an opportunity to be a loving father. He told Kevin to go to the gravesite of Nicholas and ask for inspiration to get clean and to accept his responsibilities.

Rob was insistent that Kevin had to rise to the occasion and become all he was capable of becoming. He owed this to the baby, Melanie, his family, and himself. Kevin calmly agreed to everything. He promised to visit the grave of Rob and Marla's son that afternoon. He affirmed that he understood his responsibilities. He offered no resistance and made no further comments to Rob's 45 minute motivational speech.

As Rob got up to leave, he once again elicited a promise from Kevin to go to the cemetery to receive the inspiration he needed. Kevin agreed but again offered no further comment. As we left I told Kevin that I would be over for the Giant—Cowboy football game at 7pm. He made no reply.

Of course, other than to go to the bathroom or grab something to eat from the kitchen, Kevin never left the couch until the following morning when he went to work.

I returned at night to Kevin's apartment to watch the game. It was the inaugural game of the new Cowboy Stadium, perhaps the most incredible sports venue ever built. Normally, Kevin would have been all fired up for a game of this magnitude. On this night, however, he just looked exhausted. Melanie had told me that he never left the apartment, despite his promises to Rob. He hadn't spoken to her either.

Although I wasn't leaving Iowa until Tuesday, this night was the one I had planned on to make a breakthrough with Kevin. He wasn't angry with me or rude to me in any way. We talked about the Giants and the other NFL games that had taken place during the day. Even though I assumed he was high, I was happy that he was generally peaceful and willing to talk. After all, this was the night I had expected him to see the light, come to his senses, and admit that he needed a fresh start at recovery.

As the game went back and forth, we talked mostly about football, but I got a chance to gently talk about the commitment necessary for recovery. I explained that, although he attended AA or NA meetings for a while, he never practiced the Twelve Step program. "It is a program of action," I insisted. "You actually have to **do** the steps, not just talk about them." He let me go on and on about commitment without ever really acknowledging me. I asked him if he thought he owed either Rob or me anything for all the efforts we had taken to help him. He nodded a little and quietly said, "I guess so."

With less than two minutes left, the Cowboys scored to take the lead. Eli Manning and the Giants would have one last chance to score a touchdown to beat the Cowboys in their grand debut of the new Cowboy Stadium. This was the kind of opportunity that every Giant fan lives for, to beat the Cowboys in their own stadium in a big game.

As Eli Manning methodically led his team down the field and scored with no time left on the clock to ruin the day for the Cowboy fans, Kevin had fallen sound asleep. He never saw the finish. Although he is usually the most maniacal Giant fan anywhere, his exhaustion overcame him at crunch time. The joy of beating the Cowboys would have been a great opportunity to close the deal on his return to rehab. But it wasn't to be.

****

When I called Kevin on Monday morning, he had not yet left for work. After kidding him about falling asleep at the most exciting part of a great Giant win, I asked him if he was willing to talk to me that day about rehab. He firmly replied, "Absolutely not."

After I hung up the phone, I turned to Holy Spirit and put him in charge of the day. I asked Him to carry me through the day and to use me as an instrument of His Will. I admitted to Him that I do not know what to do, but He does. I proclaimed that I was there only to be truly helpful and to be His representative. And I declared my full gratitude for my connection to Him.

I returned to Country Forest to talk to Darryl Johnson, the supervisor of the rehab facility, one more time about my options. When he suggested again strongly that he would use a "civil committal" to have Kevin brought to Country Forest, I put the process in action.

Darryl suggested that the people issuing the petition be Rob and Melanie. They were both from Iowa and would be there for the hearing. He also said that once the judge sees Melanie pregnant and the tracks on Kevin's arms, it would be a done deal.

As we were told, it wasn't difficult to get the court order to pick Kevin up once Rob and Melanie had filed the petition. Rob found out that the Davenport sheriff's office was sending two police officers to pick Kevin up at his job at the gambling recovery center downtown across from the library. I parked my car where I wouldn't be noticed but where I could watch the front door. I waited a few hours.

When I saw the police cars come and park in front of the building, I felt nervous but confident that I was doing the right thing. It took 20 minutes before they brought Kevin out to the police car. They had him put his hands against the car while he was searched for a weapon. They then drove away to Country Forest. It was 4pm.

Although I felt sad, I also felt that I did what was necessary for the circumstances. I did not want to talk to anyone about it, however. I knew Marla was preparing a big dinner but I called Rob and said that I needed to be alone for a while. I walked along the Mississippi River in downtown Davenport just thinking about everything that was taking place.

After a few hours I decided to go into the Grill Fire restaurant where I had eaten with Melanie. There was a group of about 20 people assembling in the bar before they were to go into the dining room for the 60th birthday celebration of one of their friends. I ordered a Stoli Raspberry vodka martini straight up and before long I was fraternizing with the whole birthday crowd. I had a small dinner at the restaurant and enjoyed the company of the locals at the bar.

After a second martini, I gained the courage to go outside and call Kevin's mom about what had taken place. Kevin had already called to enlist her support, so CB was a little cold when I told her all the circumstances. I told her what I did and why I did it. I explained that Kevin would not have a police record and that he needed to be clean when the baby arrived. We got off the phone pretty quickly. I didn't expect her support. CB had covered for him in the past when he stole her money, jewelry, checkbook, and credit cards. She loved him unconditionally and was not prepared to administer any "tough love" on her baby.

When I arrived at Rob and Marla's house at about 9pm, I asked them if they wanted to join me for drinks at the bar down the street. Rob's brother, Brian, was over and they had finished dinner a few hours earlier. They all gave me a big hug, put on their coats and accompanied me to the Stadium Bar about a quarter mile from their house. Melanie and a few friends joined us. I got pretty drunk but I had a good time and appreciated the strong support. I strongly felt the love that they were bestowing upon me. They are truly wonderful people who deeply touched my heart.

The next day I flew out of Moline Airport on the Illinois side of the river. Laura picked me up at LaGuardia airport in New York and we went out for dinner to discuss the events of the past few days. I was also greatly appreciative of the tremendous support I received from her. Our seven plus years of marriage had been filled with dramatic events associated with Kevin's drug addiction. She didn't know what she was in store for when she married me, but she provided the strength, love, and sound advice that I needed throughout this whole ordeal.

I knew that Melanie and Rob would be at Kevin's hearing in 3 days. The judge at the hearing further remanded Kevin to stay in the Country Forest center until he could "be released into a safe, drug-free environment while continuing with outpatient care." Ironically, it was Kevin's boss who picked him up from Country Forest the next day. When he was released it was assumed that Kevin would stay with his boss, Doug. After all, he was the supervisor of an addiction recovery center and provided a safe atmosphere. Both Melanie and Rob refused their homes to him, but Kevin convinced Doug that he could stay with a friend and the atmosphere would be safe.

I couldn't find out why Country Forest released Kevin or why Doug, an addiction supervisor, would allow him to be released without a safe, drug-free environment for him to live. Confidentiality forbade Country Forest from providing that information to me. Doug seemed unaware of Kevin's troubled past but promised me "father to father" to keep a close eye on him. Within six weeks Doug fired him.

Chapter 38 –
Kevin, Melanie, and Olivia

Melanie and Kevin welcomed Olivia Christine Glenz into the world on October 11, 2009. Kevin was there and actually cut the umbilical cord himself. Rumor has it he fled the room to vomit seconds later, but was feeling great about the birth of his daughter only moments after. Kevin immediately called his mom and she then called me. It was nice to share something joyful with CB. It had been a long time.

Days before Olivia's birth, Melanie told me that Kevin was still using and lying. His frequency of using was not as great as before but only because of the difficulty of getting heroin in Davenport and the vigilance of Melanie in watching where his money goes. There was no question, however, that Kevin was still obsessed with getting high and was depressed when he wasn't.

I talked to Kevin's boss, Doug, once a week and got mixed messages from him. In the first week, he was telling me that Kevin was improving. He said, "His attitude sucked for a few days—mad at the world—but that's to be expected. He's leveling out recently. His personality and sense of humor are returning." Doug's advice to me was firm, however, about not giving Kevin any financial help. He also repeated that he can't give me any information about drug tests because they are confidential. He also reminded me that Kevin was on strict probation but felt that he was "coming around." Doug said, "He wants the job; he wants his life. He knows he won't have either if he slides backwards." I thanked Doug and he told me to call him next week.

Doug didn't seem to realize that Kevin was still using and he was now living with a guy, Al, who drank and smoked pot all day. Al lived next door to Melanie and she told me, "Al is getting sick of Kevin fast."

I sent Kevin the following email on his work computer:

Kevin, you really do want the strength of your Higher Power to guide your life every day. You just don't think you can do that. You think you don't know how. You think that the drug can bring you more satisfaction than your Higher Power can. You are caught in an insane thought system. Take the way out that is offered you. The 12 step recovery thought system takes you right to the strength of your Higher Power in you. Dedication, commitment, devotion to DOING THE 12 STEPS is the path being offered. Peace, love, joy and happiness will never be found in that awful drug but they can be found in recovery. Dad

****

Olivia was born the next day. I'm sure I believed that she would be the motivation needed for Kevin to change. I said to Holy Spirit that I was turning it all over to Him. I know now that I was still trying to control it myself. I was making the same mistakes that I always made. I was still trying to control Kevin's addiction.

I called Doug the following week. Although he immediately congratulated me on becoming a grandpa, he seemed upset with Kevin. He said, "He doesn't seem to realize who his supervisor is. He changed his schedule on his own without informing me." He continued, "Kevin has basically used up all his chances. The next mistake could be his last." He mentioned nothing about drugs, but said, "He sure has a great looking baby."

I called Melanie. She told me that CB had arrived in Iowa to help with the baby and was staying in her small apartment. Melanie said that CB was in the shower and Kevin was at work so she could talk freely. She said that Kevin had gotten high on Friday. He had locked himself in the bathroom and Melanie knew he was in there shooting up when he refused to open the door. In her rage, she punched a hole in the flimsy panel of the bathroom door. Kevin quickly flushed his spoon and syringe down the toilet in a panic, clogging up the bathroom pipes.

It only had been 5 days since Olivia's birth and Kevin was shooting up again. After the initial wave of frustration and depression, I realized that I was getting another chance to get it right this time. I felt like Holy Spirit was telling me the old trusted AA slogan, "Let go and let God." I was determined not to condemn him or to try to control the situation.

Nevertheless, the next night Kevin called and we immediately got into an argument about his lies and drug use. Laura slipped a note under my door saying, "What are you doing? Think about what you said last night. Hang up." I realized that I was doing the exact same thing I always did. I was trying to get him to stop by heaping guilt upon him. I have known for very long that I was not to do that, but I do it again and again.

I hung up the phone and called him back later saying, "Let's start over. What do you want to talk about?" We talked about the Giants, Yankees, and Sherwood football but before long we were back on his problem. The conversation ended sadly with me saying, "If you continue to use, I really don't want to stay in contact with you."

Why can't I learn what it is I need to learn to be able to handle this? Why is my resistance to forgiveness so strong? I asked Holy Spirit to take this from me and let me think only loving thoughts of Kevin.

Kevin got fired by Doug a few days later. It was apparently over something unprofessional that Kevin said to one client in front of another. It seemed like a small indiscretion but Kevin was on probation and it was the last straw.

I texted Kevin: "Sorry for all the guilt I've thrown at u the last 5 weeks. I make the same mistakes with u over and over. I know it's tough for u."

He replied: "Thanks truly and im sorry about the guilt i throw at u over my job its just with Olivia here its really scary having no job"

I asked Holy Spirit, "Help me to help him/them in any way that You see fit."

****

I had been reading a book by Joe Vitale called *Zero Limits* about the Law of Attraction. All of the spiritual and metaphysical literature that I had been pouring myself into say, "You attract into your life whatever you think about, whether you want it or not." This message had been in all of the books I had been reading in recent years from the Hay House Publishers. Wayne Dyer, Louise Hay, Ester and Jerry Hicks, Rhonda Byrne, and many other authors in the field of personal development write about the Law of Attraction.

The basic idea is that I am not a victim of people or circumstances around me. I create everything that happens to me with my own thoughts. If my thoughts are negative, I will attract that negativity into my life. I can change my life, therefore, by reaching for the most positive thoughts that I can muster. *A Course in Miracles* puts it this way:

> "I **am** responsible for what I see. I choose the feelings I experience, and I decide upon the goal I would achieve. And everything that happens to me I ask for, and receive as I have asked." (T-21.II:2:3-5)

In this philosophy of which I am a firm believer, we are not a victim of outside forces but the maker of all that we see and become with our own thinking. Therefore, I intend on applying this to all situations that are negative in my life—but especially to how I view Kevin.

****

Before I found out about Kevin's relapse, Laura and I had planned to go to see the baby during Thanksgiving. I texted Kevin and asked if he still wanted us to come after all we went through in September. I know he resented my interference and blamed me for his losing his job. I remembered a quote from David Sheff's book, *Beautiful Boy:*

> *"Only Satan himself could have designed a disease that has self-deception as a symptom, so that its victims deny they are afflicted, and will not seek treatment, and will vilify those on the outside who see what's happening."*

Kevin was convinced that I was a control freak who wanted to ruin his life if I didn't get my way. So I was surprised when he texted back, "Yes, come. Don't u want to see ur grandchild?" And, of course, I did. He also texted, "Not getting high." Whether or not he was using drugs, he definitely wanted me to come. And that alone made me very, very happy.

For three days I got to hold my granddaughter, Olivia, for long periods of time. It's amazing how instantly I could fall in love with another human. I stared at her for hours, just wondering what her life was going to be like. Never having had any daughters or even sisters in my life, my thoughts about the opportunities for women these days took on a new meaning. Melanie was as happy as I could ever imagine with her new role as mother. She was also so happy about how baby Olivia brought our family such joy. She received so many baby gifts and warm congratulations from so many people in New York whom she hadn't ever met. And it was great to get the attention shifted off of Kevin's problem and on to the joy of bringing a new generation of our family into the world.

Thanksgiving really had no down side to it. Kevin was happy, friendly, and appeared to be sober and clean. Thanksgiving day at Rob and Marla's was fantastic. There were 34 fully eating participants between family and friends. The star of the day was Olivia Christine Glenz!

There were only a few hours over the three day period that I got the chance to be alone with Kevin to discuss, one on one, the details of my visit in September and his life subsequent to that. We took a drive down to the Mississippi River where I had spent the hours after he was picked up by police in the civil committal two month earlier. It was raining hard so we stayed in the car. The windows fogged up completely and it was dead quiet, a somewhat surrealistic atmosphere for a most important and meaningful conversation.

Chapter 39 –
Conversation at the River

———◆———

Alone together in my rented car, Kevin decided to speak honestly about his situation. I could actually feel my Higher Power telling me not to judge Kevin for anything and to love him unconditionally.

I did a lot of listening and let Kevin speak about his relapse and continuing struggles as an addict. He said his relapse took place when he returned to New York for his visit over the Memorial Day weekend in late May. He knew he could get heroin easily and cheaply and didn't believe that he would continue to use when he returned to Iowa.

Days after returning to Davenport from New York, Kevin ran into one of his roommates at Country Forest who had relapsed and had an "80 of OC" (80 mg. of Oxycontin) on him. Kevin had money in his pocket; he bought the OC immediately. Now he had a "connect".

Kevin talked about how much more difficult it was to get opiates in Iowa than on Long Island. "It's so much more expensive—the source is always so unreliable—you have to front the money, then wait hours or days—then you always wind up having to give the dealer something extra before he gives it to you," he said. He also said he didn't have a good place to shoot up. Shooting up in his car made him paranoid, but it was still the best spot. Melanie was a sleuth and finds out everything if you do it in the apartment. He said, "She's the toughest girlfriend for an addict to have."

I asked him if he did more heroin or Oxycontin. He said he always preferred heroin. The only advantage of Oxycontin was that you knew exactly what you were getting. With heroin, you never knew the quality. I mentioned that Darryl from Country Forest had said that a bunch of people have been dying from a mixture of heroin and methadone in the Quad Cities in recent months. He gave a disbelieving shrug.

But Kevin was laying it all on the line now, not just telling me what I wanted to hear. He said, "I can't get rid of the desire to be high and I don't think I ever will." He admitted that he doesn't think he can ever be happy, clean and sober and that he lacked the courage necessary for long term recovery. He said, "I see people who have been clean for ten years and they really seem happy, but I just can't imagine the early years of that being doable."

I was glad that he was opening up, but what he was saying was frightening. He seemed determined to believe that he wasn't going to be able to do it. All my efforts centered on him changing his mind about that.

He was angry still about my coming to Iowa and exposing his drug use—especially to his job at the gambling addiction recovery center. I told Kevin that I had turned that over to my Higher Power and felt I received important advice from Darryl Johnson at Country Forest. I told him everything that Darryl had told me about using everything at my disposal to get him back into recovery. "If he dies then you'll know that was God's plan and you did everything that you could to help him," Darryl said.

I also told Kevin what the lady in the sheriff's office said when we were filing for a civil committal. She said, "You understand now, Mr. Glenz, that you have done everything possible to help your son. There is nothing else that you can do." I told Kevin that I needed to hear someone tell me those words. I was so tired of trying to fix him.

I told Kevin in the car that our family might not be able to understand how he could refuse to go back into recovery after all that we had done to help him. I knew he wouldn't react well to that and he didn't. In fact, he was furious.

Kevin didn't understand why people couldn't understand what he was going through. He tried to get me to understand by making a comparison. He asked, "What is it that you love most in the world?" I wasn't quite ready for the question but I said, "I guess my relationship to my Higher Power is what means the most to me." He looked at me like that was a very strange answer.

Then he said, "Well how would you feel if that was taken away from you?" I said, "It can't be taken away." He had a look of total frustration. Thinking back on that, I wish I had answered that, "I love you most in the world, Kevin, and would be devastated if you were taken away from me."

But Kevin was trying to make a point. He believed that he loved the feeling of getting high more than anything else. I was more frightened than ever that he would never recover. He had to change his thinking or he would die, go to jail, or go insane. It was a scary moment because he seemed as if his mind was made up. He just couldn't see long term recovery in his future.

He told me that he agreed with his mother that I had a big mouth in telling others about his addiction. No one back home would think badly about him if I didn't tell them about his relapse. I told him that Al-Anon taught me "You are only as sick as your secrets." I added, "I'm not sick, Kevin." He just shook his head in disagreement.

At that point, Kevin's cell phone rang. It was Melanie. She and Olivia were outside the apartment without any keys. We had to return immediately to let them in. I wasn't ready to cut this important conversation off but we had to go.

It was an honest and open conversation—at least it felt that way. It seemed important for him to explain himself—his relapse and his current situation. Despite our differences, I knew that I was the only guy who he could really turn to for strength and candor. But how could I turn his diseased thinking around?

****

Thanksgiving Day went well without any anxiety or negative events taking place. The only downer on a very good day was that the Giants got beaten up badly by the Denver Broncos. No one in the house of Iowans really cared except Kevin and me. Nevertheless, it made the end of the night sad—as ridiculous as that may seem.

The next day before we left on the plane for home, Kevin, Melanie, Olivia, Laura, and I all went out to eat at a funky place called *The Iowa Machine Shed*. While we were waiting to be seated, Kevin awkwardly told me that he and Melanie wanted to pay for the meal, if that was okay with us. I was touched but told him it wasn't necessary. Melanie overheard it and said, "Kevin, you don't tell him that. You just intercept the check." Kevin is still like a little kid, naive in so many ways. Nevertheless, Kevin didn't intercept the check nor did he thank me for paying. It was obviously Melanie's idea.

It was apparent to me at that moment that Kevin had a long way to go. He had no commitment to recovery. He had no plan for the future in any way. There was no talk of him resuming his studies to be a radiology technician, nor plans for Melanie, Olivia, and him. He was lost. I wanted to keep the faith with positive thoughts but they were not coming into my consciousness willingly. All I felt was hopelessness.

Chapter 40 –
Christmas '09

⁂

Kevin insisted that he was coming home to New York for Christmas. Of course, he promised to stay clean. He wanted to show the baby to all his family and friends. His mom, CB, was thrilled that the baby was coming to New York and she promised to watch Kevin and "never let him out of her sight." Melanie was on board as well, although less enthusiastic than Kevin and his mom. Matthew and Jillian were excited to see the baby but they too worried about Kevin scoring drugs.

I was against the trip from the beginning but could see the upside of having Olivia with us for her first Christmas. I talked to Kevin several times between Thanksgiving and Christmas. One night on the train home from NYC, Kevin and I spoke about the Giants beating Dallas for a second time and keeping their playoff hopes alive. When Kevin saw it was me on the cell phone, he answered by singing the Bee Gees old disco hit, "Staying Alive, Staying Alive." At that moment I remember saying to myself, "I love him so much—no matter what he's doing." It was a good feeling. It was without judgment; it was unconditional. I just wish I could have done more of that thought process and less of the drug recovery conversation with which I was so obsessed.

We had a meaningful conversation on December 16, one week before he came home. He spoke of how worried he was about not having a good job and admitted that he was depressed most of the time. He spoke about the fact that he has no good friends in Iowa and how homesick he was for New York.

I suggested that he go to AA meetings and meet really nice people who would understand his situation. They would understand his depression, his cravings and maybe they could even help him get a good job. We also talked about him going back to school to resume his studies to become a radiology technician. He said the obligatory, "I know, I know" but I could tell he wasn't feeling good about anything I was saying.

A few hours later, Kevin called me back and said that he had signed up to return to college next semester for his radiology program. He also spoke about going to AA meetings but qualified it by saying, "I'm not making any promises." Still, it was a start. I was now actually looking forward to Christmas.

****

Kevin was due to arrive in New York on the morning of December 23. CB was picking the three of them up at LaGuardia Airport and bringing them to her house in Merrick. Kevin had promised to call but I received nothing from him. I called his cell at 3pm. He answered and cheerfully said, "Hey Dad, how are you?" I said, "Hey Kev, did your plane get in okay? Are you in New York? I didn't hear from you." He said, "Oh yeah, we got in fine. Sorry I forgot to call you." I could hear a lot of noise in the background. I asked where he was. He said he was at his friend's house in Sherwood. I asked how his friends liked seeing Olivia. He said they haven't seen her yet. "Melanie and Olivia are at mom's house. I just came over to see the guys for a while."

So much for CB not letting him out of her sight. He had already had her car, probably scored the heroin, and was high. But I was working on my non-judgment. Since I've learned that I project this life of mine through my own thoughts, I was determined to think only loving ones. I vowed to myself not to criticize him or his mom for lending him the car only hours after arriving. If I can change my thoughts, I can change my life. I said to Kevin, "Have a good time. I'll see you tonight."

I began to practice Ho'oponopono—the ancient Hawaiian forgiveness method of changing your mind. As this process instructs, I said to myself, "I love you. I'm sorry. Please forgive me. Thank you." I was determined to be non-judgmental—to give unconditional love. But it wasn't coming easy.

Kevin, Melanie, and Olivia all came over to my place with Matt and Jillian that night. It was obvious that Kevin was flying. Melanie had confirmed it to Laura. Kevin was all touchy-feely and bouncing around the room. I was warm, gentle, and friendly throughout the night. I had no intention of causing trouble, but I could hardly wait for him to leave. I was trying to be non-judgmental, but it didn't feel right.

I held Olivia in my arms while she slept soundly. Kevin kept hitting me affectionately as a sign that he was happy to see me. I kept asking him to stop because I had the baby in my arms. He kept asking, "Don't you love me? Don't you love me." I assured him that I did but just didn't want to be hit while I was holding OIivia.

When Kevin left to go see his friends with Melanie and Olivia, I was relieved that he was gone. Talking to him while he was high was irritating. Laura just shook her head in disappointment. He was driving high with the baby in the car. It didn't feel right to do nothing, but I backed off.

I wrote the following after doing a contemplation:

Question: How do I deal with Kevin now that it is obvious that he scored drugs as soon as he could in NY and is flying high?

My thoughts: Knowing that Kevin made no effort to stay clean when he arrived in NY, I have a terrible feeling about seeing him as well as him seeing the family (i.e.: Mike, Teresa, Stevie T, Connie, George). I know this is another opportunity for me to be non-judgmental—so I'm asking for Your help. Please help me to see this as I should.

Pray for grace, followed by meditation.
Answer: *Accept him and love him as he is. He is a projection of your own thoughts that are guilt driven. This is an opportunity for forgiveness, non-judgment. Stay with Spirit and I'll guide you. This is an important opportunity. Get it right this time. Stay with Spirit!*

****

Laura and I spent Christmas Eve with Laura's family, the McDougals. CB had Kevin and Melanie with her family at her house in Merrick to see the baby. Our plans were to see them on Christmas at my brother Mike's house and then we would all go to Stevie T's house for Christmas night.

It was a great Christmas. Kevin showed up clean and sober. Melanie and Olivia were the stars of the day. Everyone was so happy to see them and to hold the baby. Melanie was as comfortable as could be in her role as mother and she truly enjoyed being a valued part of the Glenz family.

Matt was a little bombed—but he was genuinely ecstatic about the new family dynamic. He said, "Christmas 2009 is one I will never forget. Now it all seems real; I'm an uncle, Kevin's a father, Dad's a grandpa. It's all real for me for the first time." He was truly joyous—and everyone took turns holding Olivia who looked adorable in her flowing Christmas dress.

Kevin apparently respected his uncle Mike and Stevie T enough not to show up high. That made it easy for me to enjoy the night. However, after they all went to bed, Kevin shot up and stayed up all night. At least he respected the situation so that he stayed straight until then.

Since Laura's parents had not yet seen their step-granddaughter, Kevin and Melanie promised to bring her over two days after Christmas. Unfortunately Kevin came high. I don't think Connie really knew it, but George remarked to Laura after they left that Kevin couldn't sit still for even a minute.

Melanie was upset that Kevin was high but she didn't let on to the family. She was again comfortable with Laura's parents and her brother Christopher. Kevin and Chris had been teammates for a year at Sherwood when Chris was the senior captain of the team and Kevin was only a freshman. None of us realized back then that Chris would become Kevin's uncle!

They only stayed at the McDougal house for a couple of hours but, again, I couldn't wait for Kevin to leave. I also knew Laura was upset that Kevin came to her parents' house high but she never let on. In front of the Christmas tree, we must have taken a few dozen pictures of Olivia with every possible combination of the people there. We would be very grateful to have these pictures, as things would turn out.

****

Kevin, Melanie and Olivia came to our home for a farewell visit on December 28. They would be leaving early in the morning from CB's house, so this would be my last chance to talk to Kevin face to face. I had done another contemplation the night before, and again I was told to be gentle with Kevin. *"Be gentle—show compassion—offer alternatives—but don't blame or condemn. Remember that you don't have the answers to this."* was Holy Spirit's advice to me.

I asked Kevin to take a walk with me on the Long Beach boardwalk. He appeared to be clean and sober. I told him I didn't know when I would see him again, so I asked if I could speak to him openly if I promised not to bust his balls. He agreed. I said that I knew he was high several times when I saw him over the course of the week. He replied, "What made you think that?" I said that it was obvious from his appearance, his slurred speech, dilated pupils, and how he couldn't stay still for more than a few seconds.

He said, "Melanie told you, right?" I said, "She didn't have to. You looked and acted much differently than you do now." He then admitted that he scored $60 worth of heroin when he first got to NY (it changed to $90 later in his story). Since his tolerance for the drug was low, he couldn't fool people the way he had in previous years. He said, "I only needed one bag to get really stoned, where I used to need three."

He admitted that he had every intention of getting high when he came to NY. He can't get the good stuff in Iowa. It's more expensive and awkward to score. He felt that this was his vacation and he looked forward to doing it while he was home. I know he missed the days when all of his basic needs were taken care of by his mother and all he had to do was find a way to get high each day.

I told him that I appreciated that he wasn't high when he came to Mike's and Stevie T's house on Christmas. That was when he told me that he shot up after everyone went to bed. I really wanted to talk about how he couldn't continue with this now that he had a baby. Holy Spirit, however, had told me clearly not to place blame, cause guilt, judge or condemn.

I was able to talk to him without any anger or attempt to shame him into different behavior. As a result, he spoke honestly. He said that he knew I didn't trust him to give him any money. If I could give Melanie some it would sure help out until he could get a better job. I said I would handle that with Melanie.

As we all hugged each other goodbye, I was sad because I saw little hope that anything was going to change for the better. I thought about all I had learned about how I create everything in my life with my own thoughts. If that were true, we were in big trouble because my thoughts were full of fear. As they drove away, I said to Holy Spirit in resignation, "Thy will be done, and not my own." But I could not muster up a positive thought for his future at that moment.

Chapter 41 –
Biology Book

In January, Kevin started classes again at Scott Junior College in order to become a radiology technician. Of course, I was thrilled that he was doing something so productive for his future. One day I received a phone call from him asking if I could give him $250 for a biology book that he needed for his courses. He said that I could give the money to Melanie if I didn't trust him to use it for the book. I told him that I would handle it with Melanie, but something just didn't feel right.

I had always paid for Kevin's school expenses in the past and I knew that Kevin was not making much at his new job as a cutlery salesman. I certainly approved of him taking the class and believed that the money would pay for the book, and not drugs, if I gave it to Melanie. I definitely could afford it more than they could. Still, something about it didn't feel right.

Kevin couldn't afford the book because he had lost his good job as an addiction counselor. Kevin blamed me for him losing the job. I knew that was ridiculous but that is the type of denial that is so typical of his disease of addiction. I had told Kevin that I was done "enabling" him. A definition of "enabling" could be "doing for a person what he could and should be doing for himself." If I gave Kevin the money for the book, I would be continuing to enable him. I called Melanie and explained this to her. She agreed completely, even though this would present a greater hardship financially to them.

I wrote Kevin a letter explaining why I would not be giving him the money. Before he received the letter, he called me and I explained to him then that I wasn't going to be paying for the book. He was quiet about that news and got off the phone. The next day he called and said, "I thought about what you said and I guess it is okay not to give me the money. I just don't want to lose my relationship with you. I need you, Dad. You know that. So you do whatever you think is right."

This felt good. Maybe this is a new beginning, I thought.

A few days later, I received another call from Kevin. He had just received my letter of explanation about why I wasn't paying for the book. But now, he was pissed. He said, "I can't believe you came to Iowa and caused me to lose my job. And now you think it's wrong to help me out when I'm broke and need money for school."

I said, "You lost the job because you relapsed on drugs, Kevin. You've got to take responsibility for that."

Kevin screamed, "I never would have lost it if you just stayed the fuck out of my life. You know something, Dad, I don't want to talk to you again for a very long time."

I hung up the phone. This was an old argument. I was sick of talking to him about taking responsibility for his own circumstances. Just when I thought we were making some progress, we fell back into the same old scenario.

The phone rang again. This time Kevin apologized for screaming at me. He said, "It's just that I have no money to do anything and it's scary with Olivia needing things and all."

I wish I had just accepted his apology. Instead I said, "Those are the consequences of relapsing, Kevin. You need to take responsibility for what happened and move on from here."

"Oh yeah," he said. "Let me ask you this. What would Al-Anon say about you coming to Iowa and having police take me away from my job to force me back in rehab, huh? What about, 'let go and let God?' Tell me about that, why don't you?"

I was so pissed at hearing Kevin quoting Al-Anon literature at me, I snapped back, "You know what, Kev,—let's not talk again **for a very long time.**" It would be four weeks before we would talk again on the phone.

Chapter 42 –
One Way Letters

‒‒‒◆‒‒‒

As the days went by without speaking to Kevin, I was quite upset. I checked in with Spirit to help me with my negative feelings.

Question: By refusing to give Kevin $250 for a biology book and sending him a note saying that I will no longer enable him by doing for him what he should be doing for himself, I have created some ill will between us. How do I help him from this point forward?

My thoughts: Kevin seems to have learned little from all his trials and tribulations. He isn't committed to recovery. He doesn't serve as a help to other people. He blames others (particularly me) for his circumstances. He lacks the courage to change and still wants to get high all the time.

In our last conversation, he started lecturing me on how my trip to Iowa cost him his job and how I must never do that again. I heard this before; he's ducking responsibility.

I still don't think he's learned anything from all he's gone through. He hasn't sent me a dollar to pay back what I've given. He recently had money taken out of my checking account to pay a bill—he says by mistake. He makes no effort to make amends to me or anyone. I get so disappointed by his lack of progress and feel like giving up.

I know I need to "let go and let God." I know I need to continually turn this over to You, Holy Spirit. I know I am guaranteed that You will take this feeling from me and let me see it differently. I know that I am responsible for my thoughts. I can change my thinking guided by You. Once again, I ask for Your Guidance.

> **Pray for grace—followed by meditation.**
> *Answer: You are more comfortable dealing with Kevin by letter. His voice irritates you because you associate it with his lies. Write him a letter explaining your past actions concerning trying to help (Iowa trip) by using the Twelve Step principles and Serenity Prayer as a basis for your actions. Keep your tone loving, without accusing, and full of positive vibrations that will give hope and motivate instead of causing more guilt. You are beginning to see that all efforts that use guilt to motivate are destined to fail. I am with you always in your efforts. Stay with My Guidance.*

****

I talked to Melanie the next day. She said that Kevin had been clean for a month. The last time he got high was two days after Christmas in New York when he came to show the baby to Laura's parents. Melanie also said she received the letter I sent her and the money that was a secret between us. She said Kevin's job selling cutlery was not going too well but she is not discouraging him. He was still looking for a better job. Melanie was back working shifts as a waitress at Ruby Tuesdays.

She said Kevin goes to some AA meetings occasionally. He has college classes Monday/Wednesday nights and Friday mornings. He also spends about five hours a day watching You Tube, she said. Apparently his cousin, Michael, has turned him on to that.

Kevin and I were not talking by phone but I was sending him letters. I also sent him Earl Nightengale's, ***The Strangest Secret,*** book and CD. I told him I don't enjoy our phone conversations but would continue to offer help other than money. I'm pretty sure he didn't care about my advice since it was his lack of money that occupied his negative thinking. Still, I needed to stay in contact with him somehow.

I had been reading **The Vortex** by Abraham-Hicks about the "Law of Attraction." The following quote helped me realize that I must try to stop controlling this situation and focus on controlling my own thoughts.

> **"Most people believe that control of conditions and of others is the key to feeling better, but that belief is the greatest flawed premise of all. The belief that if you could get all circumstances to change so that your observation of them would then feel good to you, defies the "Laws of the Universe," as well as your reason for being here. It was never your intention to control everything around you. It was your intention to control your thought."**

I've been spending time trying to visualize Kevin as happy and healthy. I've been trying to change my thinking by seeing Kevin, Melanie, CB, Laura, Olivia, and me all together—hugging each other in a circle with total forgiveness and love for each other.

I don't spend enough time doing that. I spend too much time thinking about how screwed up he is. I keep thinking that he's never going to make it. The drug is more powerful than his will to stop. I know I have to change my thoughts on this.

Chapter 43 –
Saturday Night Phone Calls

———◆———

It was Saturday night, February 13, 2010 when I received a call from Rob in Iowa at 8:30 pm. Laura and I were watching the video, *The Hurt Locker,* so I paused it to take Rob's call. He said, "Look, everything is okay right now but I've got some bad news. Kevin overdosed today."

I was actually calm, knowing that Rob prefaced the statement with "everything is okay." I just said, "What happened?" Rob said he got a call from Melanie saying Kevin was in the hospital. Kevin had lied to Melanie about how and why he wound up in the hospital. He lied to everyone at first but Rob eventually got the story. Rob and Marla went to two hospitals before they found Kevin recovering from the effects of a heroin overdose.

When they found him, he was angry and embarrassed to see them. He had been hoping to get out of there without anyone knowing the truth. Seeing Rob and Marla's faces was devastating to Kevin. His daughter, Olivia, was only 4 months old and Kevin had almost died. He was totally humiliated to see Marla cry. Rob was the marine who could be expected to be tough and disciplined in this situation—but Marla was different. She was the soft, loving, feminine influence that Kevin had enjoyed throughout his year and a half in Iowa. He hated for her to see him at that moment.

Rob got the story from the doctor that the police received a 911 call from Kevin's apartment about a drug overdose. Police and an ambulance arrived and revived Kevin before taking him to the hospital. Rob said that Kyle, Kevin's drug dealer, had called 911 when Kevin collapsed. Without that call, Kevin would certainly have been dead.

Rob recapped the details of the events that day with Kevin and said that he dropped him off at his apartment. Kevin was still wiped out and just wanted to sleep. I remember he was the same way after his first heroin overdose four years earlier. Rob said he would pick up Melanie from work and pick up Olivia from Melanie's mom's house. Rob wanted them to sleep at his house and to stay away from Kevin until the next day.

I told Rob that I wanted to get off the phone and give Kevin a call. Rob said that he was probably sleeping but I should try to contact him as soon as possible. I called Kevin and got his voice mail. I said that I was just calling to see how he was. I didn't mention anything about an overdose. It was my first call to him in almost 4 weeks.

Kevin called back in less than five minutes. He said, "Hi Dad, I saw you called, "What's up?" I told him that I just called to see if he was alright. He said, "Yeah, I'm alright. What do you mean?" I told him that I had just talked to Rob. He said, "Oh, okay, I figured so but I just wasn't sure that you knew yet."

Kevin's words seemed slurred and Rob told me that he still seemed high upon leaving the hospital. I said, "So it seems that you just dodged another bullet. Who called 911?" He said that Kyle, the drug dealer, did. And then he went on about how Kyle was the biggest piece of shit that he has ever come across in his seven years of being an addict.

I asked, "Did this 'biggest piece of shit' actually call the cops at the risk of being caught?" Kevin answered, "Yeah, I think he was there when the cops arrived but I don't know. They said I was still breathing when they found me—but I wouldn't be alive if he didn't call."

He continued, "Let me tell you something, Dad. I didn't wake up today ever thinking about getting high. I hadn't been high since I was in New York. Let me tell you—I've known a lot of bad people in the years that I've been doing drugs—but this guy is the biggest piece of shit I've ever come across. He called me this morning and said he needed a ride across the river into Illinois to pick some stuff up. He said he'd hook me up with some for free if I drove. You know, I knew I was doing wrong. This guy is the biggest piece of shit I've ever known—and still, I did it anyway."

I said, "Well, at least 'the biggest piece of shit you've ever known' had the common decency to call the cops and not let you die." He said, "Yeah, I guess so—but he's still a real piece of shit, let me tell you."

I mentioned to him how, when he overdosed four years ago, the guy just left him on the ground of a gas station in Brooklyn and drove away to avoid getting caught. He said, "This feels totally different than ever before. I have never been so afraid in all my life. It wasn't like this last time at all. I don't want to die—I'm telling you."

My thoughts at the time were surprisingly upbeat. This seemed like the "rock bottom" that Kevin had to hit in order to get clean. He repeated over and over how he has never been this scared in his life and that he didn't want to die. This all seemed to be a chance at a fresh start. He had been avoiding recovery but this should provide the motivation necessary—at last.

Kevin kept saying, "This all feels like a dream really. I've never been so scared. I know I don't want to die. Honestly, I don't want to die. I've never been so scared. Can you believe—not only didn't I die—I didn't even get arrested. I'm telling you this is different. I've never been so scared. I am so scared. I know I don't want to die."

I said, "Well, Kevin, it looks like Nanny is still watching over you. This should be a new beginning—a new commitment. You've got a four month old daughter now that depends on you. This is good for you. This is a new start, Kevin."

He said, "Yeah, listen—I've got to go. I haven't talked to Melanie yet. I was supposed to pick her up at the restaurant at 3pm. I told her a bullshit story from the hospital. Look I've got to go. I'll call you tomorrow."

I said, "I love you. This is a good thing."

He said, "I love you too. I'll talk to you later. I've got to go."

"Love you, bye."

"Love you too, Dad."

Chapter 44 –
Valentine's Day

‒‒‒◆‒‒‒

When I hung up the phone, I wasn't the slightest bit fearful. This was actually what I had been waiting for—some event had to shake him up enough to change. This was it. My mother in Heaven was watching out for my little boy. There really was nothing I could do to change him. Certainly I had given it my best shots for a long time. No, it would have to be something else that was totally out of my control that was going to turn him around.

There had been so many bad phone calls over the years concerning Kevin. This one gave me great hope. Tomorrow was Valentine's Day—a favorite holiday for Laura and me. I texted Melanie, "Go easy on Kevin. This is a new beginning." I told Lulu that I felt good about this.

Laura and I were having a great Valentine's Day. I called Kevin a few times but got no answer. I texted him about how I loved him and how this was a new beginning for him. Laura and I went out for a romantic dinner at a Spanish restaurant called La Rioja. We had a few drinks and were just about finishing our meal when I received a call on my cell phone from Rob.

I didn't want to answer it in the restaurant during dinner so I told Laura that I'd get back to him when we've finished. Rob called again about three minutes later. Laura told me to answer it. I thought it would be rude to talk on the cell in the restaurant. We were in close quarters and I didn't want to subject myself or others to the conversation yet. Laura, however, had a bad premonition and said, "You better call him right back. He wouldn't call twice if it wasn't an emergency." Again I said, "It can wait until we've finished eating." But Laura was upset.

The phone vibrated again a minute later, only this time it was my son Matt's fiancé, Jillian. Jillian rarely calls me. At that point I got a chill down my spine. I answered, "Hi Jillian, what's up?" She was frantic. "Please come over to the Merrick house right away," she said through a tearful, terrified voice. I asked, "What's wrong? Is it Kevin?" She just repeated, "You've got to come over right away. Please come right away."

I asked again what was wrong and she wouldn't answer except to tell me to come quickly. I said, "Jillian, is Kevin dead?" I couldn't believe I heard my voice say that. Again, she wouldn't answer but desperately begged me to come over. I asked her if Matt was there and to put him on the phone.

Matt got on the phone and in a low voice said, "Yeah."

I said, "Matt, what's going on? Is Kevin dead?"

In a very low voice, he said, "Yeah."

I snapped, "What?"

In an even quieter voice, Matt said, "He's gone." I repeated those two words to Laura. This time it was actually over. Kevin was gone.

****

I don't remember how I got off the phone with Matt or much of anything for the next few minutes. I remember that I went out back to my car to call Rob while Laura apparently paid the check. Rob didn't answer the first time I called. When I got him a few minutes later, his voice was quivering with tears. Rob just kept repeating how sorry he was.

In a high pitched, traumatized voice that was difficult to hear, he explained that no one had heard from Kevin all day. Melanie and the baby had slept at Rob and Marla's house the night before. Rob drove Melanie to work the next day while Marla watched the baby.

Rob had gone over to his apartment in the morning but the door was locked and Kevin wasn't answering the door or his phone.

Melanie was at work at Ruby Tuesdays. Finally, in frustration, Rob called the landlord who lived on the premises and told him to open the door for him because he was worried. Rob went in by himself and found Kevin lying on his back in bed. When he touched him, he was ice cold.

None of us really know Kevin's frame of mind on that last night or early morning. I was probably the last one to talk to him at about 8pm CST but Rob and Melanie had seen him snoring after that when they came in to get some of Melanie's things to take back to Rob's house.

The police report stated that he died from a lethal injection of a deadly mixture of heroin and methadone. The stuff he got from Kyle that day was bad; it was poison.

When I think back about my last conversation with Kevin, I remember how he kept repeating three things over and over. One, Kyle was the biggest piece of shit he had ever known as a dealer. Two, he didn't want to die. And three, he has never been so scared before.

Kevin had told me several times when he was in recovery that he didn't know if he would ever be able to resist the drug if it were in front of him. I remember believing him but thinking that, if he was in recovery and living in Iowa, he wasn't going to have that temptation. That fateful night Kevin obviously had the drug, the same stuff that he had overdosed on earlier. He was alone. He knew that it was a dangerous stuff. But, in his mind, there was no way he would be able to resist it.

When Kevin was telling me on the phone that he didn't want to die and he had never been this scared, I believe he knew he was going to shoot the same stuff again. Unless you're a heroin addict, that scenario seems unimaginable. There had been more than seventy drug related deaths in the area over the recent months from the same lethal combination of heroin and methadone. Kevin knew that, but he still couldn't resist. He was truly powerless over that drug—and he knew it.

Laura and I went to CB's house from the restaurant. I had not cried until I saw Kevin's mom and we both trembled as we held each other. The house was filling up with CB's family. Matt sat in the kitchen chair as if he were a stone. He was silent, angry and inconsolable. Everyone was quiet and gentle with one another. The sadness was overwhelming. We were all experiencing our greatest nightmare.

I called both my brother Mike and our best friend Stevie T on the way home. Neither answered the phone. They were out together with the wives celebrating Valentine's Day. Stevie T came right over when he found out the bad news. Both Mike and Steve had been drinking and I really didn't want any company. Nevertheless, Steve came over with his wife Rosey and my godson, Johnny, who served as the designated driver.

For some reason, I felt like I needed to print out the six letters that I had sent Kevin over the last month when we hadn't been talking. I felt that they were so important. To me, the letters represented all the love that I had for Kevin at that moment. I had been reaching out to him in that way because the sound of his voice infuriated me and brought out my worst side. I couldn't stop crying as I read each letter. Wasn't there something in those words that could help turn him around? Didn't he know the unconditional love that I had for him? Wasn't I guided by Holy Spirit to reach him in this way?

I wondered what he was thinking when he was reading my letters. Could he tell how much I loved him? Was he frustrated by my efforts to get him to embrace recovery? Was there some other strategy that I could have used to save him?

I spent the night reading my letters to Kevin over and over again. Kevin didn't write back so I was left with a one way conversation. Then I realized—I could talk to Kevin now. He was now spirit and was accessible to me through prayer and meditation. This kind of thing might not work for everyone, but I needed it to work for me.

I could definitely feel Kevin's love flowing into my heart. He wasn't angry but he also wasn't apologetic. He was loving. He was gentle. And he was letting me know that he was with me. After a while, the Xanax that Laura gave me must have kicked in. I slept straight through for 8 hours.

Chapter 45 –
A Light Born of Love is Never Extinguished

W hen I woke up the next morning, it was Monday. Laura had already been up for a while. I remember our warm embrace when we first saw each other. We didn't say much for a while but we both felt overwhelmed that, indeed, last night actually did happen. Kevin was gone. What happens now?

We talked about whom we had to contact and what steps we had to take as far as the funeral was concerned. We needed to talk to the authorities in Iowa to find out when and how we could get Kevin's body shipped home to New York. The Davenport police also had a lot of questions about the death and the drug dealer who delivered the heroin to Kevin.

Many of my friends from Sherwood HS had just left with their families on the Winter Break and wouldn't be home for another five days. I needed to stay in close touch with CB about any plans we made about the funeral.

But I didn't want to do any of those things. I just wanted to sit there and continue to think about Kevin. I wanted to go into prayer and meditation and talk to him. I didn't want to have to talk to many people about his death. Still, I knew that was what I would be doing for a long time.

I had an appointment at noon with my Pathways of Light facilitator, Sharyn. I was taking courses from Pathways to continue strengthening my understanding of *A Course in Miracles*. Sharyn and I had shared a great deal about Kevin. She also had a daughter with a drug problem. We had spent hours discussing how to handle our situations with our kids and had both turned to Holy Spirit for answers.

When I called to cancel the appointment, Sharyn was obviously shaken by the news of Kevin's sudden death. I told her that I had a lot to do concerning funeral arrangements and that I appreciated all her love and guidance. A few hours later Sharyn called me back.

She said, "Larry, I just had to call you back. I was so upset by the news about Kevin that I turned to Spirit and asked how I could help." What Sharyn said next was the most important message that I could ever receive.

She said that Kevin came to her in her meditation and told her that he wanted me to know how incredibly free he was now. He told her that the "aching, gnawing cravings for the drug that constantly haunted him" were now all gone. "Tell my dad that I'm free. And tell him that I'm happy. He needs to know." All the agony of being a heroin addict was gone. Kevin was completely free!

Kevin knew that I wasn't ready to hear it yet from him directly. He knew Sharyn was the perfect messenger to deliver that to me. When I told this to Laura, we both cried. But these tears were different from the others; these tears were of joy.

****

Once the Sherwood school community was alerted to Kevin's death, the word spread quickly, far and wide. I must have received a call from someone every five minutes that week. I'm sure many of them wished that I wouldn't answer so they could just leave a message of condolences. Calling a guy who has just lost his son to a heroin overdose is a tough call to make. No one knew what to say, so I soon developed a method of putting them at ease so they wouldn't have to speak much. I told each one that I recognized that the phone call was difficult to make. I explained that I knew there were no words that could be said and that the phone call alone said it all. I'm sure they were all relieved to be able to get off the phone quickly and I hope they felt the same love from me that each one of them gave me by making that call.

In fact, the response to Kevin's death was overwhelming. Kevin's body wouldn't be ready to come home for four more days. Each night our small condo on the beach was filled with people from all the years of our lives. We received loads of food and drink, as well as many people who just wanted to hold our hand, hug and kiss, and share many stories.

I am sure that I never understood the power of love from others as well as I did that week and for the months to come. It seemed to come from so many sources—both expected and totally unexpected. Former players of mine from as far back as thirty or more years ago came to our door and joined our family over the first three days and nights—too many to count and all of them filled with love and compassion. Since most of them knew me better than they knew Kevin, most of the conversation was about the good old days. Although they most certainly picked up our spirits, Laura and I wanted Kevin's friends to come over and talk about him.

When word was sent out that we wanted to see Kevin's friends, they showed up on the third night in full force and stayed until I finally had to kick them all out after midnight. I'll never forget the laughing, crying, and hugging of all those 27-28 year old men that night. The stories about Kevin were hilarious but we all felt a sense of loss so great that the emotions were busting open in every corner of each room. One of his friends had his high school jersey, #11 in green with gold numbers, and gave it to me. We all decided together that Kevin would want to be wearing that jersey during his wake and funeral.

We consoled each other and entertained each other with stories. The overwhelming consensus of all his friends was that "all Kevin ever really wanted was a hug." So that is what we gave each other all night—hugs, hugs, and more hugs. The love of family and friends is absolutely indispensible in a time of tragedy—and we were immersed in an ocean of love throughout the week.

Rob and Marla came in from Iowa with Rob's mother, brother, Kevin's girlfriend Melanie, and their daughter, Olivia—now four months old. We had family come in from Florida, California, Arizona, West Virginia, Vermont, and upstate New York. One of my favorite former players, Mike Morgan, owns a local Holiday Inn and put up all Kevin's family members at no charge for as long as they wanted to stay. When the family members insisted that they pay something, they were told that Kevin was part of their family too and refused to accept any payment. This type of generosity seemed to be the rule of the day.

Over a thousand people passed through the door of Perry's Funeral home during the Friday / Saturday wake and funeral service on Sunday. His coaches and teammates from NU came from all different parts of the country. The large room in the funeral home was adorned with six large poster boards of pictures of Kevin with his family and friends at different stages of his life. A giant poster of Kevin scoring the first goal of the 2000 New York State Championship stood next to his casket. He was wearing his high school jersey, number 11 in green and gold. He had the logos of his beloved Yankees and Giants along with an incredible photo of his daughter, Olivia, with him.

My recollection is that the wake was full of enormous sadness. The funeral service, however, was truly uplifting. With the help of a friend of mine, Rev. JoAnn Barrett who is a multifaith minister and teacher of *A Course in Miracles,* the service was filled with greater spiritual energy than I have ever experienced.

Hundreds filled the rooms and hallways of the funeral home to see and hear personal stories about Kevin from his coaches, friends, and family. Certainly those who came but didn't know Kevin well came away with a clear understanding of the abilities, personality, and passion that Kevin demonstrated during his life.

I was the last of the speakers. I explained how I felt Kevin's spirit hovered around me at that moment saying, "So what are you going to tell the people about me now, Dad?" I told the crowd of about 300 that Kevin had fought and lost a seven year battle with opiates. I know Kevin's mother was not prepared for me to make that announcement but I wanted the truth of Kevin's story told.

I quickly mentioned Kevin's efforts at recovery as well as his relapses. Most importantly, I spoke of how greatly I loved him and have forgiven him. I told all the people there to forgive him too. And then, like the others who had spoken before me, I told stories about him that made people laugh at this time of great sorrow.

I was overwhelmed by the energy of love that permeated the room on that Sunday morning. There would be no burial on that day because Kevin's body was being cremated. The service ended with Rev. JoAnn describing how Kevin's spirit was now joining with God and how he was "doing it so beautifully."

At no time in my life have I ever felt the love of God as strongly as then. It had now been a week since Kevin's death and I could actually feel Kevin's spirit free from his body and his disease of drug addiction. Kevin's spirit had been truly liberated. I could feel what *A Course in Miracles* teaches; that there is no death because the spirit is, indeed, eternal. Kevin no longer suffered the anguish, pain, and fear that accompanied his drug addiction. I silently thanked God for bringing that experience to my awareness at that time.

As our family and many friends left the funeral home to meet for lunch at our favorite place, the Treehouse Sports Cafe, I was filled with joy instead of grief. I was so appreciative to all the powers that be for Kevin's final sendoff to be so inspiring. I was allowed to feel tremendous love throughout the day and night and to appreciate all the individuals who made sure that I felt their love for Kevin and our family. The title on Kevin's funeral program read, "A Light Born of Love is Never Extinguished." I knew in that moment the absolute truth of that sentence.

I believe it must be a little unusual to feel such love and joy at such a moment in time. But right then I knew without question that Kevin would be with me—locked safely in my heart forever. I felt only great gratitude throughout that day and night.

Chapter 46 –
Lessons from the Grave

At Kevin's grave, he lies with his grandparents, Phyllis (Nanny) and Marshall, as well as his great aunt, Muriel, and great grandparents, Ethyl and George, who adopted my Dad back in 1920. A big, old, cherry tree hovers over the headstone in Greenfield Cemetery in Hempstead, NY.

I don't know if I've ever loved anyone more than Marsh, Phyllie, and Kevin—all buried here. But I've been taught clearly by *A Course in Miracles* that there aren't different kinds of love—just God's Love.

I've also been clearly taught that there is no death. As radical as it may sound to this world of which we are dreaming—it is a metaphysical Truth. The form certainly changes but the Spirit is eternal and changeless. It always was and always will be. Spirit was never born and can never die.

So I'm being told as I sit here in front of the grave that I know better than to get caught up too heavily in the sadness of Kevin's passing. Kevin is not really dead but has changed form. His story was one of the ego's best tricks. When sometimes I find myself reliving the horror of Kevin's death and falling into deep despair, I hear Kevin's voice say, "Hey big shot, what's the matter with you? You know better, Dad. You can't fall apart now—not after all that you've learned."

It makes me pause; and I have to answer him truly, "Yes, Kevin. I most certainly do know better than to think your 'story' was who you really are."

Kevin, you are pure Love—only Love. And I feel it. As I sit at this grave, all I feel is powerful Love. For some reason, I've been blessed to "know better". I will feel that Love deep inside my heart every time I turn to Holy Spirit because that is where you are. And Love is what you are.

A Course in Miracles teaches that we are all at home in the Oneness of God's Love—but dreaming we are in exile. Kevin is with me as he is with Holy Spirit. Until I wake up from this dream world, I will feel Kevin's love guiding me in all I do. And I feel great gratitude.

****

There also seems to be a healing among people from all sides of Kevin's extended family. It seems any grievances that anyone had for another person in Kevin's life have been forgiven and let go. No one wants to pass blame or condemnation around to anyone else. Kevin's tragedy seems to have had the message that we really don't want anything but love for each other.

We are in this human experience, so we are going to make mistakes. Nevertheless, it's clear that everyone now wants to be kind and loving to each other. That wasn't always the case. We can feel that Kevin wants us all to heal.

Before Kevin died I was trying to visualize all of us—Laura, CB, Matt, Jillian, Melanie, Kevin, Olivia, and me—all embraced in one big group hug. Kevin's friends told me, "All Kevin ever really wanted was a hug!" Although Kevin didn't make it into the form of that picture, his Spirit has united us all in a way that wasn't true before.

The best way for me to honor Kevin is to connect to Spirit. Kevin talks to me that way and I love having him with me. Turning to Universal Inspiration is where all of the strength comes from to live this experience of life as a happy dream. It depends on which teacher I choose to listen to—the ego or Holy Spirit. I'm asking Kevin's help on making this decision to choose Divine Guidance—and he will not let me down. I feel this with certainty.

A Course in Miracles teaches that forgiveness is the greatest aid Holy Spirit gives us to live happily. My forgiveness of Kevin and our forgiveness of all grievances that we hold for anyone else is the key to happiness. We are all innocent Children of God. When we see this in others, we will see it in ourselves. Forgiveness, *A Course in Miracles* style, means letting go and letting God. It is the key to living!

I ask Kevin to help me to understand these spiritual truths. I give great gratitude and appreciation for being allowed to feel all this love. My only regrets come from the times that I used shame and guilt to try and get Kevin to change. I was advised against it by Spirit and it never worked.

I can't give people advice on how to save their loved one from the consequences of drug addiction. But I encourage them to love them despite the obvious heartache. *A Course in Miracles* tells us that Love is the only thing that is real in any situation. My experience has clearly told me that only the Love matters.

> *"There is no death because the Son of God is like his Father. Nothing you can do can change Eternal Love. Forget your dreams of sin and guilt, and come with me instead to share the resurrection of God's Son. And bring with you all those whom he has sent to you to care for as I care for you."* (ACIM Manual for Teachers, C:5-6:9-12).

Chapter 47 –
Dear Kevin

⟫⟫⟫⟶◆⟵⟪⟪⟪

February 14, 2011
  Dear Kevin,
  Wow! It is one year now and I certainly have spent a lot of time thinking of you. Kevin, I'm really very grateful for our 27 years together . . . the most difficult ones included. If I want to learn the power of forgiveness, non-judgment, tolerance, honesty, and gentleness—I need a challenging curriculum. You remain my greatest teacher.

The love we shared was the only part of that story about us that was actually real! The rest was like a video or a play. It was the ego's dream that gripped us in fear and never let go. You are free of that addiction now, Kevin. I know and feel that. The spirit is eternal. It never dies.

I remember your struggle with opiates and how you didn't believe step 2 of the 12 steps: "Came to believe that a power greater than ourselves could restore us to sanity." And you resisted doing the 12 steps because the drug had a greater pull on you. I always thought that someday you would feel your Higher Power speaking to you.

It wasn't meant to happen that way. Still, for me, having two beautiful sons has been my greatest pleasure on earth. The tragedy of your passing, Kevin, can help others—maybe many others. Who knows? I have learned that only the love matters in any situation on earth.

I have some great memories of us. Some so beautiful they make me cry. One of my favorites was trick or treating with you on Halloween at age two. You were dressed as a "Pound Puppy" and no one could possibly have been cuter. You walked around holding my pinky finger while I was dressed with a frightening Batman mask. Everyone who answered the door looked adoringly down at you and said, "Awww". Then they looked up at me and their face changed to fear or discomfort from my mask. Each time they cringed looking at me, you would start laughing . . . and then so would they. It happened at every door we went to and you loved it each time.

You have taught me, Kevin, to never hold a grievance against another. Any grievance stops the full awareness of Love's Presence. I forgive myself for my own projections of fear and guilt that cause the world I see. I give great gratitude for the powerful love that comes to my heart when I call on you—like right now.

You provided a lesson for me in learning non-judgment. I read a quote recently from Gabriel Garcia-Marquez: "A man has the right to look down on another only when he is reaching to help him up." *A Course in Miracles* teaches that everything is either love or it is a call for love. Things in this world are not as they seem.

"Letting go and letting God" was the advice of Holy Spirit to me throughout the 7 years. Sometimes I just couldn't follow it. And each time I made you feel guilty, it hurt us both terribly.

Throughout it all, my boy, we've maintained a great and powerful love. I know you are there with me for the rest of this adventure, this dream of being a separate body in time and space. So, let's do some good together. What do you say?

Forgiving both me and you for whatever we experienced is the key to a happy life. Putting my life into the hands of Spirit by asking His Guidance at all times is my function. I accept it. Please, Kevin, help me to be true to it. All is forgiven.

Love, Dad

APPENDIX

ACIM and AA:

There are many similarities between these two spiritual paths, *A Course in Miracles* and Alcoholics Anonymous. Whatever differences exist between them is really unimportant when it comes to the problems associated with addiction. The 12 Steps of AA teach that you are powerless over alcohol or drugs without a connection to your Higher Power. In AA, we make "a decision to turn our will and our lives over to the care of God as we understood Him." As a student of ACIM, I have been taught that this is the greatest spiritual decision one can make. I must make no decisions on my own. Rather, I can turn to my Higher Power, Inner Guidance, Spiritual Teacher, Higher Self, Holy Spirit, Universal Soul, or any other name for this connection to your Creator.

If I don't turn to my Higher Power and stay with the thought system of the ego, I will continue to make mistakes and suffer. In both spiritual systems, I will get another chance to "do it right" if I put my will and my life into the hands of my Higher Power. Mistakes are not sins. They are errors that need correction. "A Power greater than ourselves," says Step Two of AA, can "restore us to sanity." In both systems, one prays "only for knowledge of His will for us and the power to carry that out" (Step Eleven of AA).

Turning to one's Higher Power strengthens a person in more ways than just getting clean and sober. For this reason, Kevin's drug addiction could have been seen as a blessing rather than a curse. It is the horror of heroin addiction that eventually brings one to his knees. "Admitting we were powerless" (Step One of AA) is the first step to gaining the greatest and most powerful "Friend" we can ever have. With this strength, handling the world's problems becomes much easier.

I know I would not have seen the enormous power in the Twelve Steps of Alcoholics Anonymous if I had not first had a spiritual awakening. Both philosophies recognize that we are powerless without the strength of our Higher Power. Many agnostics have found that connection to "God as we understood Him" through AA. Both ACIM and AA were divinely inspired paths that came about in the 20th century. The "Big Book" of Alcoholics Anonymous was originally published in 1939 by Bill Wilson. His experience that led to this program is believed to be divinely inspired. *A Course in Miracles* was originally published in 1976 and was "scribed" by Helen Schucman and is believed to be a modern day revelation from Jesus.

Both spiritual paths are non-denominational. People from all religious faiths and no faith have found a stronger connection to their Creator. Both paths depend on attraction rather than promotion of the ideas. They do not own a great deal of property or depend upon a hierarchy of officials for their continued existence as do the organized religions. Both AA and ACIM are studied in small groups around the world and are not allied with any religious sect or political group nor do they support or oppose any causes. The only qualification for AA is that the person has a desire to stop drinking or drugging. There are no qualifications for ACIM but it is usually found by a person looking for "a better way".

AA has a much larger following all around the world and is specifically focused on helping alcoholics and drug addicts recover. The Twelve Steps of AA are used today to help cure any addiction including gambling, overeating, and sexual obsessions. ACIM is much less popular but is growing constantly. Thousands of small groups have arisen spontaneously and can be found all around our country and are spreading throughout the world. Its intention seems to be a large scale correction for the "errors" found in other teachings of Jesus, as well as the rest of this world's spiritual systems. Its future growth in its desire to help heal mankind cannot be predicted.

Most important to me is that my spiritual path, ACIM, in no way contradicts the spiritual concepts that make AA a healing force for millions worldwide. My intention is not to promote ACIM to the reader. I do need to explain how my strong faith led me to embrace the core concepts of AA. This is a personal story of drug addiction and its true intent is to help others in dealing with this problem.

I attended Alcoholics Anonymous (AA) meetings with Kevin and found them to be inspiring and fascinating. The program of AA is for the alcoholic / addict. However, the Twelve Step program that is best designed for the parents or loved ones of a drug addict is Al-Anon.

Al-Anon:

I had heard about Al-Anon meetings but I never believed that they would be something that was for me. First of all, I have been around big drinkers and drug users all my life. I never thought I would need a support group to help me deal with someone else's addiction. I figured, "I don't need help, the addict needs help." Al-Anon was described to me as a bunch of women sitting around crying the blues to each other about their husband, son, or father. Guys like me don't go to these kinds of things. I'm a tough guy, I thought. I came to realize that Al-Anon people can be some of the toughest people I could ever meet.

So for the first five years of Kevin's opiate addiction, I never went to an Al-Anon meeting. I did go to parent meetings from one of the local out-patient rehabs to which Kevin had been forced by me to go. Although the people involved in running the meetings for the parents of drug addicted children were knowledgeable and professional, they did not focus on the spiritual aspects of the Twelve Steps. The professionals at this rehab emphasized that I had to use my "leverage" to force my son into an inpatient rehab or the disease would get progressively worse. Kevin had already been to one 28-day inpatient rehab program and left against my will and medical advice after 18 days. More expensive programs and programs of longer duration such as 90-120 days were recommended. Some of these programs cost $40,000 and, of course, no one could guarantee that it would work. I forced Kevin into several rehab centers and believe now, if the patient is not ready to be cured, it doesn't matter how cheap or expensive the treatment is. Kevin certainly was not ready.

Still, the professionals told me it was my job to fix my son by using the weapons at my disposal. I had control of the money for his college education and I owned his car. His mom also had leverage in that she owned the house he lived in and paid for his cell phone. CB had some personal knowledge of rehabs from her family history and did not have much faith in their efficacy.

Al-Anon told me something very different. After five years of slamming my head into a wall trying to fix Kevin's worsening condition, I was ready to listen. Al-Anon taught me the "3 C's." "I didn't cause it. I can't cure it. And I can't control it." That is a different message—one I would not have been able to hear a short time earlier.

I believed in some way I had caused Kevin's addiction. It must have had something to do with my life style, my divorce from his mom, my lack of strict parental supervision, or something I did or did not do. Alcoholism and addiction were deeply rooted in the family. At the very least, I was responsible for either carrying the sperm of the disease or marrying his mother with a family history of the disease. If I had been a better parent in some way, this would not have happened. I believe other people felt that way as well. I could almost read their thoughts saying, "If he was less interested in having a grand old time and more interested in watching his kids, he wouldn't have a son that's a junkie."

Curing the disease was also my job, I believed. I needed to be able to motivate my son to have the discipline and the will power to refuse to be an addict. Certainly the kid can be educated to see that drug addiction will lead him to ruin. I need to get him into the right rehab—the longer the duration, the more likely he will not relapse. I've got to keep him away from the triggers that will lead him back to using. I have to teach him about the value of surrendering to his Higher Power. I can go to meetings with him to reinforce the 12 Steps in his lifestyle.

And I most certainly needed to control the situation. I have the leverage of paying for his college costs and I own his car. I have to convince his mom to kick him out of the house, making him homeless and more likely to turn to a program of recovery. If he doesn't test clean over a period of 6 months, I should not send him back to school and he will be without a car. Hopefully his cell phone will be taken away by his mom. I have got to get CB in line with my thinking so she can help control his lying and stealing.

For more than 5 years I tried to fix this problem. When I finally realized that I was powerless to fix it, I surrendered the problem to my Higher Power, the Holy Spirit. I learned from Al-Anon that I would be able to live happily whether or not Kevin was shooting heroin. When I went to the Holy Spirit in meditation, I continually heard the same message. "How do I know what Kevin needs to go through in his life? This is Kevin's life to succeed, fail, or just get by. I'm not in charge of this situation. Trust the message of the Holy Spirit and get out of the way." A key slogan of AA and Al-Anon is "Let go and let God." I was ready to do that. I said, "Holy Spirit, how do you see this? I quiet my mind and open to Your healing perception."

At Al-Anon meetings family or friends of the addict share their "experience, strength and hope" with each other. It is believed that if you "keep coming back," and "listen", you will hear what you need to hear. You will be given tools with which to have serenity in the midst of turmoil. But Al-Anon with the Twelve Steps is a program of action. You actually have to do things, not just sit and listen. I have to make "a searching and fearless moral inventory" of myself (Step Four). I have to admit "the exact nature of my wrongs," (Step 5) and ask my Higher Power to "remove all these defects of character (Steps 6 and 7). I have to make "a list of all persons I had harmed" (Step 8) and make "direct amends to such people wherever possible" (Step 9). I have to use "prayer and meditation" (Step 11) and "carry the message to others" (Step 12). It doesn't work unless you actually DO the steps. It is a program of "action".

Law of Attraction:

The metaphysical *Law of Attraction* is not a new concept to me but in the fall of 2009 everything I was reading and studying seemed to be focused on this concept. The basic idea is that:

> You create everything in your life with your own thoughts. You become what you think about.

> And there are no exceptions to this; it is Law. It is not a new spiritual thought. In fact, it is truly ancient dating back to the earliest of Hindu teachings. This can be interpreted in different ways, of course. *A Course in Miracles* teaches that everything in this world, except Love, is a projection of the ego mind and is, therefore, an illusion—a total misperception. ACIM teaches us that the belief that we are separate bodies is a mass illusion. We are all at home united in the Oneness of God, but dreaming we are separate and in exile!

> Although the *Law of Attraction* was familiar to me for years, it was becoming clearer with every reading. Joe Vitale's book, *Zero Limits*, demonstrated that the ancient Hawaiian spiritual practice of Ho'oponopono taught the same concept—your thoughts create everything that you see. A specific process was developed to "clean" your thoughts. Changing how you see the world changes what you see in it.

> *The Vortex,* by Ester and Jerry Hicks explained more clearly to me that my thoughts create a certain spiritual *Vibration* that will attract what it is aligned to from the Non-physical or Spiritual world. In short, if my *Vibration* is focused on what I don't want—more of what I don't want is attracted. I must, therefore, train my mind to reach for the highest *Vibrational* thought available to me in order to attract what I really do want.

Since I wanted to attract a clean and sober Kevin Glenz, I needed to get rid of the fearful thoughts with which I had been surrounding myself for the past seven years. If I am obsessed with fearful thoughts, I will attract fearful things. Therefore, I started to spend time visualizing Kevin, Melanie, and Olivia in a happy family scene—hugging and kissing each other in a loving embrace. I had to visualize Kevin speaking in front of an AA meeting of many people as a devoted, grateful addict in recovery.

As I look back upon this, I realize how much time I had spent thinking such fearful thoughts. "He can't get anything done." He won't commit to a program of recovery. He doesn't want to be clean and sober. He just wants to get high above all else."

Few of my thoughts projected success for Kevin compared to my enormous fears of Kevin dying or going to prison. One of my darkest thoughts was about Kevin being in prison and wanting so badly to get high that he performed sexual favors for heroin. And some of my fears were even worse and involved him in violent crime. If one believes that the Law of Attraction is true, it is important to take a good look at what your thoughts are and to change them if they are fear based.

Because Kevin has died from a heroin overdose, it is difficult to think that I caused that with my own thinking. That belief could cause serious guilt if perceived wrongly. If the story of my life and the lives of all these other bodies in the world I see is all illusion, Kevin is and always has been at home in God. His life story and all our stories are not real. Everything I see with the body's eyes is a projection of my own ego thoughts. Only the love is real. I cannot change any of my past thoughts but I am in control of what I think "now". "Now" is the only part of eternity that is real in this dream of time and space.

The love for each other that Kevin and I experienced during his lifespan was real. It still is. It is a reflection of God's Love. I carry that love with me now. Kevin is spirit. His love will guide me with more focus on Divine Guidance than I have ever been able to muster before. I do not plan on dwelling in the darkness.

As Kevin is reminding me when I turn to him, "You know better, Dad. You know only the love is real and the rest was just an illusion projecting from the ego thought system. Don't throw away all that you've learned, Dad, now that your faith is being tested. My love will guide you every second if you allow it."

I truly do hear that voice. It has the inflection, biting sarcasm, and humor of Kevin at his best. But now it contains something new. It contains Wisdom and Truth—the power of Holy Spirit.

Forgiveness—*A Course in Miracles* style

Forgiveness is the cornerstone of the teachings of *A Course in Miracles* (ACIM) but it is not like the traditional thoughts about forgiveness. In traditional forgiveness, the forgiver lets go of his grievance of another but still believes the other has done something wrong. I might add that people who practice traditional forgiveness usually believe that there are some things that are unforgiveable.

In ACIM, forgiveness of any perpetrator of perceived wrong-doing is essential. ACIM teaches that nothing in the world is as it seems. In God's eyes all his children are innocent, sinless, and created exactly like their Father. In the world of form they may do terrible things. But the world of form—this world we think is so very real—is actually an illusion, a dream, a video, a play.

What you see in the world comes from your thoughts—not your body's eyes. When you change your thoughts to align with those of the Holy Spirit, what you see in the world changes. Therefore, when you forgive another for his perceived transgressions, you are actually forgiving yourself for your own projections of your own wrong-minded thinking. The result is healing. Wild, isn't it?

This book is not intending to convince anyone about the metaphysical teachings of ACIM. But it teaches that the power of forgiveness is the greatest aid we have to achieve personal happiness while we believe we are a body here on earth. Forget about understanding the metaphysics of an illusory world if you are not ready for that belief. But unless you are ready to forgive others of what you perceive to be their sins, you cannot heal yourself.

If you choose to hold on to any grievance at all—no matter how convinced you are of its justification—you will suffer the effects. Deciding that you want to hold on to a grievance against another is like pouring gasoline on yourself, lighting yourself on fire, and then hoping that the one whom you're mad at suffers from smoke inhalation. It's insane. And, according to ACIM, this is true 100% of the time. No exceptions!

This belief that you will suffer if you hold on to any grievance, ranging from a mild irritation to a deep-seated hatred, is essential to healing. Forgiveness is the tool that we have while in this human form to achieve happiness and peace. Holding a grievance is self-inflicted punishment.

If you become determined to convince yourself or others of the guilt of another person or people, you will deny yourself the opportunity to think like God. If you learn to forgive others, no matter how heinous their sins appear, you will experience only God's Love.

We have the freedom in every moment to choose for the ego or Holy Spirit. The teacher you choose makes all the difference.

LAST FIVE LETTERS
WRITTEN TO KEVIN
12/30/09
1/19/10
1/26/10
2/1/10
2/8/10

December 30, 2009

Dear Kevin,

Your mom called me to tell me you guys all arrived home in Davenport safely. Obviously your trip to NY had its good and bad sides for me. Wonderful to see a beautiful mother and child that are now part of our family; sad to see you still struggling.

The part that is most meaningful to me was when we were out on the boardwalk talking on the last day. You told me you don't get the "Higher Power" stuff. And I know that is true and honest. If you did or when you do—EVERYTHING CHANGES. But it all starts with changing your mind—and only you can change YOUR MIND.

The first thing that is holding you back from making this big change is "the fear of failure". You don't want to go through all the recovery effort and fall back to square one with a relapse and let yourself and others down. It has been said by the professionals that relapse is part of recovery. Something important is learned by every personal failure—BUT NOT IF YOU GIVE UP.

Let me make an effort here to explain the Higher Power stuff. Calling it God just does not work for a lot of people—so it is referred to also as "Higher Power," "Inner Guidance," "the Universe," "Divine Inspiration," "Sacred Friend," "Holy Spirit," "the Source"—whatever feels right.

And this POWER is not "out there" but inside of you—inside YOUR MIND—ready to be tapped into in order to live a life of meaning. I know you don't believe that now—or at least you don't believe you have access to that source of strength. And even if you do believe there is a Higher Power waiting to help you, you think it will fail you or you will fail it in the long run.

THAT'S WHY THE MOST IMPORTANT THING IS YOUR ABILITY TO CHANGE YOUR MIND!

You might be asking yourself now, "How do I change my mind? It doesn't seem to want to change. It just wants to get high all the time! It keeps telling me that getting high is the greatest feeling in the world." And that's true. That is what your mind is telling you right now. BUT IT IS LYING. Your mind needs healing.

First of all, the greatest feeling in the world is LOVE, not heroin. Not physical love (although that feels good too) but emotional / spiritual love. This love starts with loving yourself. Without question, you need a connection to the "True Spirit" within you to really love yourself.

The good news is that your Inner Guidance waits for you until you are ready. It is always there, even when you are fucking up left and right—waiting for you to be ready to turn to it. You can't lose it ever—but you can ignore it—AND YOU ARE IGNORING IT. You don't even believe it is there. You think you're all alone in your struggles against the world—including your addiction. All this time YOUR HIGHER POWER IS WAITING FOR YOU TO COMMIT TO IT.

I have told you many times that I know that you have been taught about the importance of COMMITMENT in getting anything done. I know you understand that. So your biggest problem is that YOU DON'T BELIEVE YOU CAN DO IT.

You don't think you can stay with a commitment to recovery. You don't think you can enjoy a life of sobriety with AA people. You don't think you can become an honest, trustworthy, productive father, lover, brother, son, and friend. And now you are afraid to try again. Your mind (which unfortunately is sick—has a disease) is telling you that nothing will satisfy you like heroin. It is telling you that you would rather be a heroin addict than be of value in a world of people you love.

It is a disease that you have—a disease of the mind. Many others share this disease. Some never heal—they die early, go to jail, or become insane. Others find a connection to the Spirit inside of them through a COMMITMENT to a plan of recovery.

- You have never made the commitment.
- You have never done the 12 steps (I know your Uncle Danny did).

- The strength to recover comes from connecting to your Higher Power.
- The Spiritual Awakening (belief in a Higher Power) comes from doing the 12 steps.
- Devotion to attending AA meetings is the start (devotion being the key here).
- The 12 step program helps you to CHANGE YOUR MIND.
- The people in AA will become more meaningful friends than any you have ever had before.
- There is a life of great joy and meaning in your future with recovery.

You might be telling yourself, "I want to believe all this—but I don't." I know. But there is help out there in AA. Step 12 says it all. "Having had a spiritual awakening as a result of these steps, we tried to carry this message to others, and to practice these principles in all our affairs."

YOU ACTUALLY HAVE TO **DO** THE STEPS. Not just go through the motions of attending meetings. Right now you don't believe it will work, so you just sit on the couch and watch television—miserable unless you are high. You think all you need is a job right now. That is part of the disease. Nothing will go right without a commitment to recovery.

You can do it! YOU CAN CHANGE YOUR MIND. You and only you can save your own life and help the lives of others immeasurably. Years of doing drugs have destroyed your confidence in yourself and damaged your self image. YOU CAN DO IT! Take the help and commit. No one can do that for you. There is a great life waiting for you, Kevin.

Love, Dad

January 19, 2010

Dear Kevin,

When we last spoke, you were down. Somehow money was coming out of my checking account by accident? You were apologetic, but you were feeling badly about yourself and your circumstances. You can stay feeling down and depressed as long as you want. When you're ready—AND ONLY WHEN YOU'RE READY—there is help.

Right now you have no good energy inspiring you. Your thinking is the cause of all your problems—not anything that is going on in your world.

You think:

- You just need a good job.
- You just need to be able to get high without your whole world falling apart when you do.
- You don't have what it takes to turn your thinking around.
- You have no connection to the Source of all strength.

I know you think these things and have been thinking them for a long time now. You have a sick mind that needs healing. Your thinking is the cause of your problems—nothing else. Therefore, my beautiful son, you have to CHANGE YOUR THINKING!

The best way for you to change your thinking is total devotion to attending and participating in meetings—like every day or night— no excuses. By joining with others in an effort to help each other, you help yourself. Service to others is a healing process. Helping others is therapy that always works.

But your biggest problem is not your disease of addiction— not your lack of a good job—not your depression over your life circumstances. **Your biggest problem is your resistance to accepting the help that is waiting for you when you are ready.**

AA is not the only path to a connection to your Higher Power—but it is a proven method for people with your particular problem. I found my own path when I was at my lowest point—and it made all the difference.

HOW MUCH COMMITMENT WILL IT TAKE TO COMPLETELY TURN YOUR LIFE AROUND? You might ask. But you really know the answer to that—and still have great resistance for some reason.

- Going to a meeting every day shows commitment
- Actually DOING the 12 steps at step meetings and at home shows commitment.
- Speaking up or sharing at meetings about your thoughts shows commitment.
- Meeting regularly with your sponsor shows commitment.
- Calling your sponsor when you have craving shows commitment.
- Reading AA literature for spiritual support shows commitment.
- Volunteering to help the group members and others shows commitment.

What baffles me is how you can think your life now is preferable to that commitment I just described. The satisfying job, the happy living situation, the loving family situation, the meaningful friendships—all this can be gained for connecting to the Source of all Love. The 12 steps are one path of many that leads to that connection. Devotion to that path costs little in money, contains cool people who understand your particular problem, and has proven to be successful to those who totally commit.

My commitment to you is total—but I know now that I need to let go and let God. I will encourage you with as much love and emotional support as you are willing to accept. I will not enable you by helping you to do the things you need to do for yourself. Your mom has good loving intentions when she gives you money but she has kept you thinking as a dependent child as a result. I won't do that anymore because I know you need to do it all yourself.

Sending me $5 a month as a symbol of your desire to pay me back and to straighten out your life is a powerful motivator. Include a short note of love and gratitude and it completely changes your entire energy field. Doing something kind and thoughtful for Laura—such as a call, card, text message—changes your energy to one of thinking of others. Doing similar things for your mother, brother, Olivia, Melanie, Maureen, Marla, and Rob all change your energy field.

If you're still not ready to accept and embrace this type of thinking that I am describing, I will wait until you are. Letting go and letting God means not forcing my way on you. I know that I am a good example for you to follow. My advice is solid but means little to someone insisting on remaining sick.

You are and have been experiencing whatever you need to. If you find the strength to be successful in recovery, you will be a source of strength to many others. You can have a greater impact on the people of this world than I have. Your story can be one that inspires millions and gives your life more meaning than you ever dreamed. BUT YOU MUST CHANGE YOUR THINKING.

Your Higher Power waits for your readiness, my beautiful boy. I love you sick or healthy.

Love, Dad

January 26, 2010

Dear Kevin,

I sent you this book (CD is the same—DVD on gold side) because I want to provide ways and opportunities to CHANGE YOUR THOUGHTS. This book or CD is not about addiction or connection to your Higher Power. It is about the power of your thoughts in determining what happens in your life. It's short and meant to be read or listened to repeatedly.

You may not be ready or willing to read or listen to the message. If so, either give it to someone else or throw it out. As your dad who loves you, I will continue to try to give advice that is meant to be helpful. I never know what will kick in with you or when. It's your life—I don't plan on interfering again but am making no promises.

As far as what Al-Anon would say about my trip to Iowa in September, I see it this way. The Serenity Prayer says:

- **God, grant me the serenity to accept the things I cannot change.** I can't change your thoughts. Only you can—but you need help—some program of mind training to change the wrong mindedness of your disease.
- **The courage to change the things I can.** I could make the effort to change the bad situation of active addiction, financial debt, a frantic expectant mother of your unborn child, and a disillusioned cousin distraught over your relapse. I needed to make the effort.
- **And the wisdom to know the difference.** I asked my Higher Power for advice. He sent me Darryl (Country Forest) who twice said, "Do a Civil Committal." No matter what you think about the importance of that job, you were going backwards into debt and you had become a fraud.

You could have handled yourself better when I came to Iowa. You could have handled yourself better after I left and Doug got you out of Country Oaks. Your diseased thinking betrays you every time. You need to change your thinking or your life will not improve. You need to take personal responsibility.

Blaming me or anyone else for your situation is part of the disease. I don't enjoy talking to you on the phone. I want to help but not enable. I believe you will turn around your thinking sooner or later. I believe in the long run, you will become the man you are capable of being. You will learn to help others and gain enormous satisfaction from it. You will become a great father, husband maybe, brother, son, and friend to many. There is a really good man inside waiting to come out. It will happen—when is up to you.

You've got work to do on yourself. There is help out there. Any success in anything important depends on you finding a program to change your thinking. Only you can make that happen. This book I sent you is just a different approach. I love you and think about you all the time.

Love, Dad

February 1, 2010,

Dear Kev,

We haven't had any verbal contact lately, but that doesn't mean that you're out of my thoughts at all. Our relationship will evolve as it is supposed to over the years to come, just like it has over the years that have passed.

My personal favorite time of us together was when you were a youth level player in Merrick and I was your coach. We weren't as good as we were together in Lynbrook, but we had more fun and things were less serious—at least for me. You were still a bit of a lunatic as I recall—but a cute one and very tough and extremely competitive.

I also loved the years of us living together with Nanny. The times were kind of chaotic exciting. Nanny was really challenged by your temperament and tendency toward disrespect—but she was a tough old broad and she thrived in the situation and was thrilled with all the action that you and I provided for her in the Sherwood years. I will always believe that the three of us moving in together in Sherwood during those years was the right thing to do—no matter what happened afterwards.

Shortly after you graduated high school, I moved out with Lulu, you went to college and lived in Merrick, and Nanny lost her mind. Certainly the years of Nanny going bad in the head and you going bad with addiction were the most difficult for me.

Other than having a dad who was determined to "cure" your dangerous drug addiction and vigilant in using all the weapons at his disposal to try and accomplish that, you had it easy in Merrick. You always had enough money to get high and always had someone give you a car, a phone, food, shelter, and freedom to come and go as you please. You came to resent me, even though you loved me. You were dependent on your mom and she accepted that—even though she complained.

I'll agree with you that you got yourself out of that situation with Rob and Marla's offer. The future looked very bright and everyone was proud of your turn around. From my view point, it was your lack of devotion to your recovery program that allowed the relapse less than a year ago. A disease like yours requires great vigilance or relapse is very likely.

The financial situation you are in now is the result of relapse, I believe. You put yourself in debt BEFORE I interfered again in your life. Since I bailed you out of thousands of dollars of bank fraud debt in the fall of 2008, I felt I had the right to come to Iowa at my own personal expense to try and turn the situation around. From my view point, it was your resistance to getting help that cost you your job. I know you see that differently—and I DON'T want to argue that point again with you.

I don't plan on ever interfering with your life again. I was thrilled to hear from Melanie that you were a month clean since your trip to NY. I truly only want to be helpful to you—but we have different ideas about what that entails.

I still think you should be paying me back $5-10 dollars a month with a note of appreciation—but you see it very differently, I guess.

You are going to make the turn, Kevin—hopefully sooner than later. I have complete faith that, as time goes on, you'll find a path that helps you change your mind about what's important in life. I know that I need to accept you the way you are—and, of course, love you anyway. And I do—very, very much. Always have—always will.

You may not agree with everything I have done concerning your addiction over the last seven years. You may not agree with how I treat you in the future. But if you think I want anything but great love, happiness, peace, and joy in your life, I assure you that thought is only a symptom of your disease.

You agree that you have a disease now. We don't agree on what it takes to handle this so that you can experience a life of love, peace, and joy. But you're a young guy and your thinking will change over time. I hope you don't have to suffer too long before that change in thinking takes place.

YOU CAN DO IT, KEVIN! But only YOU can do it. I'm rooting harder than anyone. No matter what you think now, no one is responsible for your future success except you. You can do it—and you will. It's just a matter of when. Why not now, tough guy? Why not now?

Love, Dad

February 8, 2010

Dear Kev,

I saw Matt yesterday on Super Bowl Sunday at the Treehouse and he said that he saw you, Melanie, and Olivia on a webcam with your mom's side of the family. That sounded very cool. Olivia could get to know me and see me on camera from a computer screen. The idea of that makes me happy and the fact that you are already doing that with your mom is great.

I hope the three of you are doing well together. Although I do miss talking to you about things like football and stuff, I don't miss the negativity that often comes from honest conversations between us. Now that you are a father, you might be able to see my situation better than before. I don't know. Olivia is so young and her relationship with you doesn't compare to one of two adult men as father and son. One thing you might get a new feel for, however, is the type of love that exists between a parent and child.

My relationship with my father was different than you and me, obviously. Maybe he was an easier father than me. Maybe I was an easier son than you, maybe a little of both. Times were also different. Pop didn't pay as much attention nor did any other fathers for that matter. Kids were left alone more than they were when you were growing up and a lot more than now. Maybe that was better.

I no longer look back and wonder what I could have or should have done differently. I know for a fact that Mike resented my father for much of his life. He doesn't now. When Pop was dying of cancer and my mom would bring up to him how differently he treated me than Mike, Pop would just say, "Hey, I thought I was doing the right thing." He certainly didn't beat himself up over it. After he died, Mike seemed to have completely changed his thoughts about their relationship. To my knowledge, he no longer has any resentment at all and has nothing but admiration, love, and respect for his old man.

Maybe it'll be the same between you and me. Pop died at 72; I'm 59. I may or may not live a lot longer but I don't want to wait to die for you to lose the resentment. Nevertheless, I no longer want to help support you financially—nor try to control your drug addiction. The last part, you probably don't believe. I don't even know if I believe it. But I hope it's true. I know I never feel good at all when I'm trying to control or even influence your drug use. That didn't stop me, I know, but it always felt terrible—always.

It takes time, if you ever learn, what being a good father really is. Our separation in distance and now in conversation is probably what is best for us right now. I'm sure we both know we love each other. We have had very different ideas about how each other should behave in our roles as father and son. I'll accept that. Forgive me for how I've behaved. I forgive you.

Be a good father to Olivia and a good man to Melanie—or not, if you so decide. IT IS YOUR LIFE. It's just taking me a little time to come around to that thinking. I'm working on myself all the time, but old habits die hard. I guess you already know that, though.

Love, Dad

And then he was gone and
I have written this book.
I hope that it can help you.

Matt, Phyllie (Nanny), and Kevin (2006)

Kevin, Jillian (Matt's fiancé), and Matt (2009

Kevin, Laura, and Larry (Thanksgiving 2008)

Larry, Kevin, Marla, and Rob in Iowa (2008)

Melanie, Olivia, and Kevin (Oct. 2009)

CB (Kevin's mom), and Kevin (Christmas 2008)

Acknowledgements

I have great gratitude for the people who helped me and advised me during the writing and publishing of this book. Pathways of Light minister Sharyn Zenz was the first to read my manuscript and her advice both strengthened me and touched my heart. Pathways of Light founders, Robert and Mary Stoelting, gave me further encouragement in believing that this book would help others.

Two educational administrators and friends, Dr. Santo Barbarino and Dr. William O'Sullivan, offered their wisdom and compassionate suggestions of how the book's content would be received by the parents and families of young men and women who are tempted to try illegal drugs for recreational purposes. Much of what was included or deleted in the book's content came from their influence.

My wife, Laura, read my manuscript with difficulty after having lived the events described in the book with me. Her sensitivity to the way that family and other loved ones of Kevin would be affected by my accounts of his struggles positively influenced how the difficult times were portrayed. Laura served as the family advocate to advise me on what would be too difficult for those others to read.

My great friend, Kevin Murphy, may best understand my intentions in writing this book and was my greatest resource in deciding how much of my spiritual beliefs were appropriate to include in the story.

Danielle Leighley, a former colleague and close friend, graciously helped me with technical aspects on the included photographs.

My generous friend and editor, Bill Picchioni, used his considerable skills acquired from a career of teaching high school English classes to clean up the numerous errors in grammar and style. He also had a great influence on my choices of the material included or deleted. He has become a most trusted friend.

Our football and lacrosse coaching staffs gave so much of themselves in their efforts to help me with Kevin. They were always there for us to share their love for Kevin and our family and were my closest confidantes throughout the process.

I thank all of our family and friends for the support and love that gave me the strength to complete this work. And I feel special appreciation to Kevin's mom and brother for allowing me to tell this story from my personal experiences. The torrent of love that came to us as a result of Kevin served as the motivating force to complete this book. Holy Spirit is my Ultimate Advisor; I need only the willingness to serve.

Contact info:

larryglenz@verizon.net

535A W. Broadway, Long Beach, NY 11561